THE
ROLLER
COASTER
LOVER'S COMPANION

A Thrill Seeker's Guide to the
World's Best Coasters

Revised Edition

STEVEN J. URBANOWICZ

CITADEL PRESS
Kensington Publishing Corp.
www.kensingtonbooks.com

CITADEL PRESS BOOKS are published by

Kensington Publishing Corp.
850 Third Avenue
New York, NY 10022

All Kensington titles, imprints, and distributed lines are available at special quantity discounts for bulk purchases for sales promotions, premiums, fund-raising, educational, or institutional use. Special book excerpts or customized printings can also be created to fit specific needs. For details, write or phone the office of the Kensington special sales manager: Kensington Publishing Corp., 850 Third Avenue, New York, NY 10022, attn: Special Sales Department, phone 1-800-221-2647.

First Kensington Printing: July 2002
10 9 8 7 6 5 4 3 2 1

Printed in the United States of America

Library of Congress Card Catalogue Number: 2001099100

ISBN 0-8065-2309-3

Facing title page: Loch Ness Monster, Busch Gardens, Williamsburg
(Courtesy of Busch Gardens)

Title page: Cedar Point's Magnum XL 200
(Courtesy of Dan Feicht, Cedar Point)

THE

ROLLER
COASTER
LOVER'S COMPANION

For my mother, Carolyn

The Great American Revolution at Six Flags Magic Mountain.

Contents

Acknowledgments   ix

Introduction   xi

Before We Begin Our Ride: How to Use This Book   xiv

1. From Russia, With Love   3

2. Thrill Machines, Thrill Makers   13

3. Getting the Most When You Coast   31

4. Types of Roller Coasters   37

5. The World's Best Wood Coasters   41

6. The World's Best Steel Roller Coasters   48

7. The Parks With the Best Collection of Coasters   56

8. The Guide to Roller Coasters Worldwide   61

9. The Best Roller Coaster Trips   101

10. The Top Five Roller Coaster Lists   120

Glossary   137

Index   139

The author (right) enjoys NITRO at Six Flags Great Adventure with John Griffin, Nikki Lauren, and Vinnie Mazella. (Author's Collection)

Acknowledgments

A big "thank you" to everyone involved in nurturing my love of roller coasters and amusement parks.

First and foremost, to my mom, Carolyn, who never stopped taking me to amusement parks when I was a child, just because she knew I loved them. Also, to my grandmother Jean, the true thrill seeker of the family, and my aunts and cousin Brook.

Also, thanks to my long-time coaster-riding buddies (you know who you are), and welcome to the storm, Vinnie! In memory of Richard Klimek and Michael Bent.

Many thanks to Kristin Kocher, Pat Klingensmith, and Gail Rios at Six Flags Great Adventure and Janice Witherow at Cedar Point for their help and friendship over the years.

And to all parks, manufacturers, and individuals who supplied information or photographs, I am forever in your debt.

Wild Thing, Valleyfair! (Courtesy of Dan Feicht)

Introduction

Why do we ride roller coasters? Why would people allow themselves to be lifted to impossible heights, only to plummet crazily to the ground? Who would want to careen through insane curves with their bodies bouncing around like rowboats in the Atlantic during a hurricane?

There may never be a satisfactory answer. For each and every one of us the reason we venture aboard these monstrous thrill machines is different. Some of us are looking for death-defying kicks. Others may simply be looking for a good scream. And, believe it or not, there are those who think roller coasters are just plain, honest-to-goodness fun!

Whatever the reason for coaster riding, it is obvious that the number of folks who do participate in this passive "sport" is high. Over 300 million people visit amusement and theme parks each year in the United States alone. At each and every park, the most-ridden attraction is always a roller coaster. At parks with multiple coasters, it is not unusual to find that all the most popular rides are coasters.

The parks know that coasters are what the guests come to ride, and it is not out of the question for a new coaster to be added every season or two. A brand-new wood or steel scream machine can cost anywhere from $4 million to $18 million, but it can also increase the park's attendance dramatically, sometimes as much as 30 percent, a worthwhile return on the investment.

A major thrill ride may take as long as a year to be installed. Construction and landscaping alone can add $4 to $6 million to the total cost, but the parks are more than willing to make these huge investments, as they only have to look at their profits to see the obvious: if they build it, we will come. Again and again.

For those of us who love these magnificent creations, these are truly exciting times. The race is on to build the biggest, wickedest, must stunning coaster in the world. More than fifty new rides open each season. Most are

〰〰〰〰〰〰〰〰〰〰〰〰〰〰〰〰〰〰〰〰〰〰〰〰〰〰〰〰〰〰〰

Roller Coaster Fact: Leap-the-Gap, an early twentieth-century design, featured (surprise!) a gap in the track. Trains were supposed to jump across and land safely on the other side. It never opened to the public, because it was discovered in the experimental stages that the course of the vehicle would vary depending on the weight of the passengers it carried.

〰〰〰〰〰〰〰〰〰〰〰〰〰〰〰〰〰〰〰〰〰〰〰〰〰〰〰〰〰〰〰

good, some are exceptional, and a few are legendary from the moment the train crests the lift-hill.

A good roller coaster need not be the biggest, longest, or fastest. What is important, what does make a good ride, is "pacing": that is, how the hills, turns, and speed are placed in the finished package to create the total ride experience. It takes much more than an engineering degree to build a great coaster. An acute sense of drama and intimate knowledge of psychology must also be employed.

Contrary to an all-too-common belief, roller coasters are extremely safe devices. Of course, sometimes there are mechanical problems, but they occur so rarely that one need not even be concerned about them. Serious accidents do happen on occasion, but these are almost always due to the foolish behavior of passengers. It would seem that for some, the thrill of riding a coaster is insufficient, so they attempt to enhance the experience by standing up, or switching seats, or any number of asinine antics. That Do Not Stand Up sign is there for a reason, folks. Because rules are sometimes ignored, parks have invented ways to protect riders from themselves; most coaster trains now have at least four different types of restraints. Some of these may take a little of the edge off the ride experience, but let's face it—that's an easy compromise to make to ensure that everyone makes it back to the station safe and sound, even the idiotic ones. In some states, rider misbehavior is considered a misdemeanor crime.

Regarding other safety concerns: No, coasters cannot jump the tracks; they are locked into place. No one has ever been thrown from a coaster because the ride itself was too rambunctious. Lap-bars do not fly open during the ride. Trains have never fallen apart while in motion. Even the oldest coaster has never collapsed with a train full of riders going through the course. And g-forces, all calculated by sophisticated computer programs, are all within the realm of what the human body can withstand—in fact, jumping off a chair to the floor exerts more strenuous force on the body than any

〰〰〰〰〰〰〰〰〰〰〰〰〰〰〰〰〰〰〰〰〰〰〰〰〰〰〰〰〰

Roller Coaster Fact: Among the more famous admirers of roller coasters are Matt Dillon, Michael Jackson, Natalie Cole, Kristy McNichol, and the late Vincent Price, Judy Garland, and Elvis Presley.

〰〰〰〰〰〰〰〰〰〰〰〰〰〰〰〰〰〰〰〰〰〰〰〰〰〰〰〰〰

roller coaster even comes close to. There are too many myths to count. Just keep in mind that statistics show that walking through doorways has caused more injuries than coasters. At the parks, so too have carousels. In fact, the stats also show that *getting to the park is far scarier than being in the park!*

So feel free to ride a roller coaster, with gleeful abandon. And while we'll probably never know why we do, we must like whatever it is that these monuments of kinetic sculpture provide to us. Whether it be physical, emotional, or psychological gratification (or perhaps spiritual or intellectual), between March and November, it is our season. Our time to give in to the irresistible urge to ride a roller coaster.

It is our time to take the plunge into the abyss, fully aware that we'll want to take that plunge again.

Before We Begin Our Ride:
How to Use This Book

*T*he *Roller Coaster Lover's Companion* is designed to tell you everything you need to know to get the most out of roller coaster riding.

Chapter 1 provides a brief history of coasters, detailing the types of rides that have existed since the first person rolled down a track, to the present day mega-monsters. Chapter 2 tells you about the builders of the different types of coasters you're likely to encounter in your travels.

In chapter 3, you'll discover many of the little secrets coaster enthusiasts have been privy to for years, so you can enjoy coastering more: from which seat is the best to money-saving tips on admission. Chapter 4 describes all types of coasters and coaster technology to enable the novice to better understand what he or she is getting into. (There's also a glossary at the end of the book.) In chapters 5 and 6, you'll find top lists of the best wood and steel roller coasters, respectively. The top must-visit parks with the most extensive coaster collections are listed in chapter 7.

Chapter 8 lists the important roller coasters on each continent (listed by country, then state or province, then park) and includes *The Roller Coaster Lover's Companion*'s exclusive rating system, created to help you determine if a certain ride is too wild, too mild, or just right for you. Chapter 9 recommends what parks to combine to make truly stupendous mini-vacations, all designed around coastering.

And finally, check out the top five lists in chapter 10, comparing them to the list of favorites that you yourself might have already been creating.

Now get ready to roll!!!

THE
ROLLER
COASTER
LOVER'S COMPANION

1 FROM RUSSIA, WITH LOVE

The first roller coaster, in the form that we know today, was built in New York's own Coney Island in 1884. It was a scant fifteen feet tall, and ran at a whopping top speed of four miles per hour.

We've come a long way, baby!

Today's roller coasters top out at over three hundred feet, and speeds of more than 90 mph are not uncommon. Some are made of wood, more are made of steel. Modern coasters go upside down, and even more notably, passengers enjoy them while sitting, standing, hanging with their legs dangling, or lying facing down to the ground. In short, coasters don't just go up and down any more.

While usually considered a purely American form of entertainment, these rides have their ancestry in a much more intriguing place than Brooklyn, New York, and it wasn't some carnival barker who thought them a viable diversion.

You see, the first folks to board a vehicle and roll down sloping hills for sport were guests at the Russian Imperial Summer Palace during the late eighteenth century. The person who devised this avant-garde pleasure was the palace's occupant, Catherine the Great, and even she had to get the idea from somewhere.

It was during the sixteenth century that the first ice slides were built. These were wooden structures with step ramps thickly coated with ice, and passengers took turns sliding down aboard sleds fitted with runners. A popular pastime for over two hundred years, the ice slides had only one problem—

Opposite page: The Cyclone at Coney Island, the world's #1 wooden coaster. (John West, Astroland)

they could only operate during the cold of the winter season. Catherine the Great wanted to slide during the summer as well, so she had her sleds fitted with wheels. The world has been coasting ever since.

The term "roller coaster" would find its origins in a French adaptation of the Russian ice slides. The climate in Paris proved to be unsuitable for ice slides, so ramps were fitted with rollers upon which standard sleds with runners would coast—hence, "roller coasters". This arrangement was soon abandoned in favor of grooved wooden ramps and sleds with wheels, but the name roller coaster remains in use to this day.

The rides were so popular that they inspired innovations to improve each new one built. The first rides built in both Russia and France required their passengers to climb to the top of a tower in order to embark on their thrilling journey, which consisted of a simple single in-line drop. In the early nineteenth century, the people of France built the Belleville Mountains and the Promenades Aériennes. Both rides featured cars securely locked to the track, guide rails to keep them on course, much higher speeds, and greater thrills than ever before.

Meanwhile, some thrill riding was beginning to occur in the United States as well. In eastern Pennsylvania, an eighteen-mile-long incline railway, formerly used for transporting coal, was turned into a public attraction known as the Mauch Chunk Scenic Railway. Its railroad cars were hauled by steam engine to the top of the mountain, then simply coasted back down to the bottom. A brakeman was on duty at all times to see that the speed didn't get out of hand. Traces of the Mauch Chunk Scenic Railway still exist, and the area has since been declared a National Historic Landmark.

Slides similar to the Russian and French versions began appearing in the United States, but it wasn't until 1884 that a truly historic roller coaster event took place. The Switchback Railway opened for business on 10th Street and Surf Avenue in Coney Island, the world-famous Brooklyn, New York, beach resort. Located roughly where the famed Coney Island Cyclone now resides, the Switchback Railway is regarded as the first "modern" roller coaster ever built; that is, it featured an undulating track, with vehicles seeming to defy the law of gravity as they coasted over these hills. Legend has it that LaMarcus A. Thompson, the Switchback's inventor, was a Sunday school teacher and preacher, who created this milestone attraction to divert young men from frequenting the beer gardens that were popular at the time.

Whatever his reasons, the ride was enormously popular. It consisted of two side by side tracks, and passengers had to climb to the top of a platform to board the train. It was pushed out of the station and came to a stop at ground level some 600 feet down the beach. There, passengers would climb to the top of another tower (sometimes they had to help push the car up there,

A "coasting party" at Coney Island. (*Frank Leslie's Illustrated Newspaper,* July 24, 1886)

too), where the vehicle would be switched to the return track and pushed out for the return trip. An oval-track roller coaster debuted at Coney Island later that same year without these undesirable features.

In 1885, the first full-circuit coaster with a lift-cable was built. Philip Hinkle's Gravity Pleasure Road became the most popular attraction at Coney Island and started a wave of roller coaster construction across the country.

Not to be left out, LaMarcus Thompson began building coasters that included dark tunnels with painted scenery in them. His first, the Oriental Scenic Railway, opened in Atlantic City, New Jersey, in 1886. At the time, he patented his attraction. Since that day, all roller coasters built in the United States have been referred to as "scenic railways" by the U.S. Patent Office.

By 1900, Coney Island had the first looping roller coaster. It was built entirely of wood, and featured a single, completely round loop, which would viciously snap riders' heads, causing whiplash. The Flip-Flap, as it was known, attracted moe viewers than riders, and its single two-passenger car did not allow the ride enough capacity to make money. The head-snap problem was solved soon afterward on Loop-the-Loop, one of which opened in Coney Island, the other in Atlantic City. The shape of the loop was changed from the perfectly round circle to an ellipse, or teardrop-shaped (clothoid) loop. Passengers sailed throught he inversion with nary a physical complaint. Unfortunately, single cars kept the capacity down on these rides as well, and they became financial failures. Looping roller coasters would not be built again until the 1970s; capacity problems were solved, and building material had changed from wood to steel, but the shape of the loop would be the same teardrop configuration used in the early part of the century.

Roller coasters were being built everywhere during the early 1900s. The usual desing for the rides at the time was a figure eight, with gentle dips the main thrill. Cars would run freely on the multilevel track, with wooden guide rails keeping the vehicle on track. A prime example of this type of ride still exists at Lakemont Park in Altoona, Pennsylvania. A National Historic Landmark, Leap the Dips is the oldest operating roller coaster in the world.

As the race to build the biggest, most thrilling roller coaster continued, it was soon discovered that existing methods of construction and safety features were dramatically insufficient. John Miller is generally regarded as the father of the modern roller coaster, as it was he who added to the cars wheels that ran under the track, keeping the trains in place during high-speed drops and turns. Miller also developed the locking lap-bars, anti-rollback ratchets, and other safety devices that are still in use on today's coasters. Without John Miller's inventions, we would not have the wild thrill rides of today. Miller designed rides featuring high humps, one after another, all with steep drops A good example of a John Miller ride still operates at Six Flags Worlds of Adventure in Aurora, Ohio, a Cleveland suburb. Known as the Big Dipper, it is one of the oldest operating coasters in the country, and a prime example of the wildness that can be found in what is by today's standards a small roller coaster.

With the advent of Miller's inventions, any type of design could now be executed. Near-vertical drops, heart-stopping spirals, and vicious trick-track became the order of the day. The Roaring Twenties was the Golden Age for among other things, roller coasters. Literally thousands were built, each attempting to outdo the last in size and thrills. Frank Prior and Fred Church

Raging Wolf Bobs is based on the Bobs at Riverview Park in Chicago, which closed in 1967. (Courtesy of Geauga Lake)

built Bobs coasters—spiraling, swooping scream machines. One of these, the Airplane at Playland in Rye, New York, is regarded as the greatest roller coaster ever built (sadly, it was torn down in 1957, but the park has an interest in rebuilding it). In fact, of the many rides Prior and Church built, only two still operate, and only one is truly indicative of the typical Prior and Church design—the Giant Dipper at Belmont Park in San Diego, California.

Similar to Bobs designs were Harry Traver's Cyclone Safety Coasters. These rides also featured the spirals and swoops found in Prior and Church's Bobs coasters, but each was pitched much more severly, with some 85-degree banking not uncommon. Traver built only four Cyclone Safety Coasters. Three were removed rather quickly, but one, the Cyclone at Crystal Beach, Ontario, Canada, lasted twenty years (closing in 1946) and was known as the most frightening roller coaster ever built. Legend has it that a full-time nurse was on duty in the loading station at all times. The Cyclone and the Rye Playland Airplane are the two roller coasters that any serious fan of roller coasters would wish he or she could go back in time to experience.

The severe nature of 1920s roller coasters can be experienced today to its fullest effect on the Cyclone at Coney Island, New York. Built in 1927, this National Historic Landmark, although not truly indicative of the swirling masterpieces built during it's time period, features all the steep drops and tight roughhouse curves a roller coaster lover could want. It is the mother of all existing wooden roller coasters, and the one ride that all other coasters are measured against and aspire to be as good as. A restoration currently underway is making the Cyclone ride much as it did when it was brand new.

Although coasters continued to be built, the Depression spelled the end to the widespread construction of the 1920s. During that time, many parks closed, and their roller coasters were torn down. With the onset of World War II, followed immediately by the advent of television, roller coasters rapidly began to disappear. Two thousand roller coasters worldwide dwindled down to two hundred. Amusement parks became shabby, shady operations, and poor maintenance led to safety hazards. No one cared about parks anymore; people had found other things to do with their leisure time.

But in July, 1955, an event took place that would signal the rebirth of the amusement park: Walt Disney opened Disneyland, the nations first "theme park." Six Flags followed in 1961, opening Six Flags Over Texas in the Dallas –Forth Worth metroplex. The arrival of the theme parks (of which forty to fifty were built in the ensuing twenty years) coincided with the final operating season of some of the nation's greatest amusement parks, including Chicago's Riverview and northern New Jersey's Palisades Amusement Park. But one thing was very clear. The parks that survived would likely prosper,

Cyclone, Coney Island, New York. The 1927 original is still one of the most thrilling rides in the world. (Courtesy of Bobby Nagy)

and the new theme parks were a hit. Along with this renaissance in parks came a rebirth of the roller coaster.

This time, however, things were different. Disney and Six Flags built roller coasters using a new type of tubular steel track. Disney's Matterhorn, opened in 1959, featured a smoothness of ride and a deafening silence never before experienced on a coaster. When Six Flags debuted its Runaway Mine Train, there was incontestable proof that the roller coaster was back—but in an altered form. Coasters were now designed to attract families, and nothing in the ride was too severe or frightening, so no family member, from the youngest to the oldest, would hesitate to ride.

Soon that would change. At exactly the time that the Palisades Amusement Park Cyclone came crashing down, a new wooden roller coaster was under construction at a brand-new theme park outside of Cincinnati, Ohio. When Kings Island opened in 1972, so did the Racer, a dual-track master-

The Kings Island Racer heralded the return of the wooden roller coaster. (Courtesy of Paramount's Kings Island)

〰〰〰〰〰〰〰〰〰〰〰〰〰〰〰〰〰〰〰〰〰〰〰〰〰

Roller Coaster Fact: A bizarre fashion trend during the 1960s was the disposable paper dress. One woman found out just how disposable these frocks were when she wore one on a coaster. During the ride, the wind tore the dress off her, and she arrived back in the station stark naked.

〰〰〰〰〰〰〰〰〰〰〰〰〰〰〰〰〰〰〰〰〰〰〰〰〰

peice designed by John Allen. The Racer is widely known as "the second coming," for it created a great deal of interest in the giant roller coaster again, and spurred a building boom in large wooden roller coasters. Six Flags followed the next year with the Great American Scream Machine in its Georgia park, and the race was on once again to build the longest, tallest, fastest and best roller coaster in the world. The title holders have changed almost every season since then.

But something else was happening in the world of roller coasters. Almost simultaneously, two California parks, Six Flags Magic Mountain and Knott's Berry Farm, opened steel looping coasters, the kind that have become the mainstay of today's parks. Knott's Roaring Twenties Corkscrew featured a double upside-down spiral, while Magic Mountain's Great American Revolution soared passengers through a single 360-degree loop. Ever since, all hell has been breaking loose!

For many reasons, theme parks have become places to take inexpensive mini-vacations, so they have remained extremely popular. Most of the older, smaller parks have also been doing quite well. The revenues generated have enabled park owners to invest what at times seem to be insane amounts of money on new thrill rides. Through all of this, the roller coaster has remained the most popular attraction at the parks, so in the time since the amusement park revival, we've seen more incredible forms of thrilling roller coasters built than that old Switchback inventor LaMarcus Thompson could have ever dreamed of.

The 1970s finished in a big way with the Beast at Paramount's Kings Island, which at 7,400 feet is still the world's longest wooden roller coaster. The single loop of Magic Mountain's Revolution has given way to the eight-inversion screamfest Dragon Khan at Port Aventura, in Tarragona, just outside of Barcelona, Spain. In 1984 was the world debut of the stand-up roller coaster, the King Cobra at Paramount's Kings Island, as well as the first successful suspended roller coasters, the Big Bad Wolf at Busch Gardens in Williamsburg, Virginia, and the XLR-8 at Six Flags Astroworld, in Houston, Texas. The 1980s ended with the first coaster ever to break the 200-foot height barrier, the Magnum XL-200 at Sandusky, Ohio's Cedar Point. In

~~~~~~

Roller Coaster Fact: The Lake Placid Bobsleds at Palisades Amusement Park in New Jersey was the world's tallest roller coaster when it opened in 1934. Only a few seasons after it was built, the ride was torn down. The Bobsleds, however, held the record for the world's tallest coaster for nearly forty years. Until the debut of the Beast at Paramount's Kings Island iin 1979, no coaster had been built that was taller than the Bobsleds 125-foot height.

~~~~~~

1992, Batman–The Ride came on line as the first inverted, outside-looping, chair-lift-style coaster.

As we approached the new millennium, linear induction motors came into play, launching roller coasters to new heights, at speeds of 100 mph, doing away with the traditional lift-hill clattering of the past 110 years. New ways to ride included a lay-down flying coaster (Stealth, at Paramount's Great America, in Santa Clara, California) and the world's first floorless coaster, Six Flags Great Adventure's (Jackson, New Jersey) Medusa—a ride with trains best described as kitchen chairs attached directly to the wheels. And, the first full-circuit coaster in the world to break the 300-foot barrier opened at Cedar Point. Aptly named Millennium Force, the ride caused an immediate sensation. Meanwhile, during all of these amazing technological advances, new wooden roller coasters like the Texas Giant, Hershey's Wildcat and Lightning Racer, and the Roars of Six Flags America and Six Flags Marine World have been built in the grand style of the 1920s, and have been instant hits.

And to think, all of this, because someone wanted people to find something better to do with their time than drink beer!

2 THRILL MACHINES, THRILL MAKERS

Every roller coaster ever built works on a very basic scientific principle: what goes up must come down.

It is this simple law that is used to design all roller coasters. The force of gravity dictates the height of every hill after the initial lift-hill, and inertia determines how long the track length can be, depending on the height first attained by the structure.

In the days before computers and ultra-scientific equations, roller coaster builders designed their rides in a rather seat-of-the-pants manner. They would build their ride, and if the train of cars did not make it through the complete circuit, they would adjust hill heights accordingly.

This relatively unscientific approach sometimes resulted in rides with exceptionally high g-forces. Small "rabbit hop" hills positioned immediately after larger deep dips would occasionally produce severe "negative g's," lifting passengers up out of the seat. These moments, which roller coaster lovers refer to as "airtime," occur because the heavier train is being rapidly pulled down a hill while the much lighter passenger is still being projected in an upward motion. While today's computer-designed coasters still frequently provide these thrilling weightless moments, they are much less severe and much more controlled. For a good example of negative g's at their unbridled best, try the Comet at The Great Escape in Lake George, New York. Originally built in 1946 at Crystal Beach Park in Ontario, Canada, this masterpiece was constructed in the days before computers dictated how much a roller coaster could throw the passenger around in the car. The Comet was relocated to the Great Escape in 1994, with no changtes made to its design, and it features airtime on each and every hill.

The Comet also contains many moments of lateral gravity. Old-time

〰〰〰〰〰〰〰〰〰〰〰〰〰〰〰〰〰〰〰〰〰〰〰〰〰

Roller Coaster Fact: The Coney Island Cyclone has inspired no fewer than six copies currently operating worldwide: Texas Cyclone at Six Flags Astroworld; Georgia Cyclone, Six Flags Over Georgia; Psyclone, Six Flags Magic Mountain (California), Viper, Six Flags Great America (Illinois); White Canyon, Yomiuriland, Tokyo, Japan, and Wild Wild West, Warner Bros. Movie World, Germany.

〰〰〰〰〰〰〰〰〰〰〰〰〰〰〰〰〰〰〰〰〰〰〰〰〰

roller coasters quite commonly featured turns that were designed flat and were taken at high speeds, slamming passengers sideways to the outside of the turn. On some rides, this would cause passengers to collide with each other or, at the very least, careen into the side of the roller coaster car. On the more severe rides, broken ribs would not be surprising. The Great Escape Comet features several of these lateral slamming moments; fortunately, none of them are of the rib-breaking variety.

Today, computers determine the degree to which negative and lateral gravity will affect the passenger. If the results in a computer model are too severe, the coaster designer can lower the hill or bank the track more extremely. Coaster trains are also now equipped with lap-bars that prevent the passenger from lifting out of the seat too precariously, and most rides now have seat dividers to keep side-to-side movement at a minimum.

No matter how computer-controlled these devices get, in the long run, they still work the same way the roller coasters of yesteryear did. On a recent excursion of mine to an amusement park, weather conditions and an insufficient number of passengers to weight the train properly caused one roller coaster train to stop dead at the top of a hill, stranding passengers in a driving rain a hundred feet in the air. While this was a modern ride, built with all the new-fangled computer technology we now possess, the solution to the problem was quite primitive: maintenance works had to climb the structure, attach a cable to the train, and winch the train over the hill so that it could continue along the circuit. That is, in the end, the beauty of roller coasters. No matter what magical gadgetry is attached to them, they inevitably operate in the same way they have for over one hundred years. Gravity still rules the day; track and wheels, in basically the same configuration as on 1910 coasters, are still standard; a simple link-chain still gets the train to the top of the highest hill; and the screams of the passengers haven't even come close to changing since the first passenger boarded the Switchback Railway in 1884.

THE BUILDERS

It's hard to believe that such primitive devices could cost $18 million or more, or that so many very successful companies would be in the business of building them. But that's the cost for a large, modern scream machine, and builders of today have attained an almost celebrity status. For roller coaster enthusiasts, the famous designers of the past are saints.

Philadelphia Toboggan Coasters

The Philadelphia Toboggan Company, opened in 1904, has built some of the best wooden roller coasters in the world. The father of the modern roller coaster, John Miller, designed some of his earliest works for the company. Miller's protégé, Herbert Schmeck, followed in the master's footsteps with sharply pitched hill designs producing negative g's similar to those of Miller's coasters. Schmeck designs still in operation include the Yankee Cannonball at Canobie Lake Park in Salem, New Hampshire, and the Phoenix at Knoebel's Amusement Resort, Elysburg, Pennsylvania (the Phoenix was originally known as the Rocket, operating in Playland, San Antonio, Texas, until its relocation to Pennsylvania in 1985).

John Allen became PTC's chief designer during the 1950s, and he is the man most responsible for the roller coaster renaissance of the 1970s. His Racer at Paramount's Kings Island (1972), Great American Scream Machine at Six Flags Over Georgia (1973), and Screamin' Eagle at Six Flags St. Louis (1976) were each responsible for a new wave of roller coaster fever. Allen not only knew that a ride had to be thrilling, but he also understood the esthetics of roller coaster design—to this day, his rides remain some of the most beautiful pieces of amusement park sculpture in the world.

PTC—now known as Philadelphia Toboggan Coasters, and under the direction of Tom Rebbie and Bill Dauphinee—continues to be a major force in the roller coaster business. While the company no longer designs or builds coasters, it is responsible for the manufacturing of roller coaster trains, station air gates, and other vital equipment. Today, trains made by PTC are in operation on almost every wooden roller coaster in the world.

The John Miller Company

John Miller, (formerly of PTC) founded Miller and Baker with Harry Baker in 1920. In 1923, the pair split, and Miller formed his own company. Rides from his company still operating include all three wooden roller coasters at Kennywood in West Mifflin, Pennsylvania. Miller later partnered with Norman Bartlett to create the Flying Turns, a trackless roller coaster whose trains ran freely within a carved-out wooden trough. Several of these rides were built in the 1930s, the largest of which, the Lake Placid Bobsleds at New Jersey's Palisades Amusement Park, was considered the most frightening. Its 125-foot lift-hill gave it the distinction of being the first roller coaster to be over 100 feet in height. Although the ride closed in 1946, another roller coaster approaching that height would not be built until 1979: Kings Island's Beast. No Flying Turns rides still exist, but modern incarnations of this type of ride can be found at several parks, most notably Paramount's Kings Dominion in Virginia. The park's Avalanche, although built of steel, closely reproduces the experience of the older ride.

Harry Baker's company, meanwhile, is responsible for the building of the world-famous Cyclone at Coney Island. Today, the Cyclone is still in operation and is one of the best roller coasters in the world.

Harry Traver
Prior and Church

Both Harry Traver's Cyclone Safety Coasters and Prior and Church's Bobs design, discussed in chapter 1, were renowned for the "spiral dip"; that is, a turn during which a drop is executed. While none of Traver's frighteningly severe rides still exist, two Prior and Church coasters do. The Giant Dipper at Belmont Park in San Diego, California, is indicative of the spiraling nature of these designers' signature creations, while the other, the Dragon Coaster at Playland, in Rye, New York, is not. Dragon, although an extremely long ride, was built as a milder alternative to the pair's infamous Airplane, considered by many to be the greatest roller coaster ever built. Its flat turns and shallow drops still offer thrills, but not the kind that Prior and Church normally provided.

Arrow Dynamics

The first steel roller coaster to achieve star status was Disneyland's Matterhorn. Built in 1959, it was the first to use a tubular steel track, and Arrow was the company responsible. Arrow went on to develop the family-style mine train coasters that became prevalent at the theme parks during the 1960s. The company is also renowned for introducing a ride that has become a staple at nearly every park in the world: the log flume.

Arrow really took the amusement industry by storm by being the first to reintroduce the concept of looping steel roller coasters to a world ready for a new way to be thrilled. The company's Roaring Twenties Corkscrew debuted in 1974 at Knott's Berry Farm in California. It topped out at a height of 70 feet, and during the course, riders were flipped upside down during a double spiral. The coaster currently operates as the Gravity Defying Corkscrew at Silverwood Theme Park in Athol, Idaho.

Paramount's Kings Island Vortex, installed in 1987, is a good example of how truly twisted Arrow Dynamics's looping coasters became. (Courtesy of Bobby Nagy)

After this historic debut, Arrow continued to build larger, more dramatic variations, soon incorporating 360-degree loops, double-flipping boomerangs, and direction-changing sidewinders. Although the company's looping steel roller coasters would eventually approach 200 feet in height, they still incorporated the same inversion elements made popular during the 1970s. Among Arrow's most thrilling looping coasters are the Loch Ness Monster at Busch Gardens in Williamsburg, Virginia, the Vortex at Paramount's Kings Island in Cincinnati, Ohio, and the Great American Scream Machine at Six Flags Great Adventure in New Jersey.

Arrow introduced the suspended roller coaster in 1984. Trains on this type of coaster hang below the track and swing wildly with every turn. Among the best are the Big Bad Wolf at Busch Gardens in Williamsburg, Virginia, the Ninja at Six Flags Magic Mountain in Valencia, California, and Top Gun, a movie-themed extravaganza in Cincinnati's Paramount's Kings Island.

The company ended the 1980s in a big way. Cedar Point in Ohio had asked the company to build a large, traditional profile roller coaster out of steel: traditional in that it would feature no loops, corkscrews, etc., but instead the more familiar deep drops, camel backs, and rabbit hops that had characterized smaller wooden roller coasters for a century. While it started out as a 180-foot-tall project, it soon grew to 205 feet, becoming the first roller coaster in the world to ever break the 200-foot barrier. The appropriately named Magnum XL-200 is still the park's most famous ride, and its tranquil setting along the shores of Lake Erie belies its rambunctious nature. From beginning to end, the ride is ferocious—an experience totally without finesse, designed to produce hard-core thrill after thrill.

Arrow went on to build other non-looping steel giants, among them the Pepsi Max Big One at Blackpool Pleasure Beach in England and Desperado, a 209-foot-tall behemoth that operates as an alternative attraction at Buffalo Bill's Resort and Casino in Stateline, Nevada.

Arrow's newest project is known as X, at Six Flags Magic Mountain in California. Riders sit in four-across vehicles, two seats on either side of the track, with legs dangling, and each two-passenger vehicle rotates 360 degrees forward and backward during the course. The ride is a 200-foot-tall monster, with a first drop that is 90 degrees straight down.

Togo International

The Togo company of Japan has been in the amusement business longer than Arrow, building all types of amusement rides in its native country. In the United States, the company caused a sensation in 1984 with the debut of the world's first looping steel coaster to have its passengers ride standing up: the King Cobra at Paramount's Kings Island (Ohio). Similar rides soon appeared at Paramount's Kings Dominion (Virginia) and Paramount Canada's Wonderland (Ontario).

The company next introduced Ultra Twister at Six Flags Great Adventure in New Jersey, in which six-passenger vehicles were pulled up a 90-degree lift-hill to a height of 97 feet, only to plung down an 85-degree drop (still one of the world's steepest drops), then execute heartline spirals both forward and in reverse (on a transfer track). Ultra Twister now operates at Six Flags Astroworld, in Houston, Texas, modified with a still steep 45-degree lift-hill, but retaining the steep first drop and multidirection heartline spins.

In 1988, the company built the Bandit, a huge non-looping terrain steelie. With a lift height of 167 feet and a vertical spread of 256 feet, it became the world's tallest coaster and perhaps served as inspiration to Arrow and Cedar Point for the following year's Magnum XL-200.

1995 saw the debut of the mega-coaster, a standard steel roller coaster capable of negotiating in-line spirals. The world's first installation went on line at Six Flags Great Adventure and is known as the Viper. A much larger variation opened at New York New York Hotel and Casino in Las Vegas. The

Great Adventure's Viper, and an example of a heartline spiral. (Courtesy of Six Flags Great Adventure)

Manhattan Express is 203 feet tall and features a standard loop as well as a heartline flip; its cars are designed to look like little yellow taxis.

Anton Schwarzkopf/Intamin, AG/Werner Stengel

German designer Anton Schwarzkopf, the principal designer for Intamin, AG, was also in the business of building amusement rides well before he made a big roller coaster splash in the 1960s, when he designed and manufactured what has become a very familiar sight at most smaller amusement parks and traveling carnivals. His Jet Star, Wild Cat, and Jumbo Jet compact portable steel models, most in the 50- to 60-foot height range, are still popular among roller coaster fans.

Schwarzkopf began installing larger, permanent rides based on Jumbo Jets in the 1970s. Generically known as speed racers, they send four- or five-car trains with tandem seating along several thousand feet of twisting turning track, all computer-designed to allow passengers to ride safely without the need for a lap-bar. The only version still operating in the United States is the Whizzer at Six Flags Great America in Gurnee, Illinois.

Not to be outdone by Arrow Dynamics, Schwarzkopf introduced the looping steel coaster in 1976. The Great American Revolution at Six Flags

Twenty linear induction motors put to their best use with the Wicked Twister at Cedar Point.. (Courtesy of Cedar Point)

Magic Mountain in Valencia, California, was the first modern roller coaster to feature a 360-degree loop. Other Schwarzkopf looping coasters currently in operation are the Six Flags Over Georgia Mind Bender (still one of the world's best looping steel roller coasters), Shockwave at Six Flags Over Texas in Arlington, and Texas Tornado, at Six Flags Astroworld (Houston). Anton Schwarzkopf's looping coasters are distinguished by the fact that, although extremely smooth, they are designed with wooden roller coaster attributes, like negative and lateral g's, and can operate with just a single lap-bar (although several also feature unnecessary over-the-shoulder harnesses).

As Anton Schwarzkopf retired (passing away in 2001), a new designer took up where the man hailed as the "father of the steel coaster" left off. Werner Stengel is now responsible for designs for not only Intamin, but most of the greats built by several other companies as well, and he works both in wood and steel. His non-looping hypercoaster designs include the Superman Ride of Steel attractions at various Six Flags parks, hailed as several of the

One of Anton Schwarzkopf's U.S. masterpieces is the triple-looping Mind Bender at Six Flags Over Georgia. (Courtesy of Bobby Nagy)

world's best roller coasters, and Son of Beast, at Paramount's Kings Island in Ohio, currently the world's largest wooden roller coaster, at 218 feet tall, and also the world's only looping wooden coaster!

Charles Dinn and Curtis Summers

Although Charles Dinn and Curtis Summers operated two separate companies, the Dinn Corporation and Curtis Summers, Inc., their collaborative efforts, with Dinn as the builder of Summers designs, resulted in some of the great wooden roller coasters of our time.

Charlie Dinn burst onto the roller coaster scene in a huge way. He was responsible for building Paramount's Kings Island's Beast, which is still the longest wooden roller coaster ever built. After he formed the Dinn Corporation, his first projects involved moving older wooden coasters from parks that had closed to new parks that had purchased the rides. This task had rarely been attempted in the past, but Dinn changed all that. His relocation of the San Antonio, Texas, Rocket to Knoebel's Amusement Resort in Pennsylvania is considered miraculous. Dinn was also to work miracles with the Lakemont Park, Pennsylvania, Skyliner (moved from New York State) and the huge Giant Coaster, formerly located at Paragon Park outside of Boston, Massachusetts. The Giant, now known as the Wild One, is happily rolling along at Six Flags America in Largo, Maryland, and is the tallest wooden coaster (98 feet) ever to be moved from one park to another.

Dinn first teamed up with Curtis Summers on a completely new design with the Wolverine Wildcat at Michigan's Adventure in Muskegon and the Raging Wolf Bobs at Six Flags Worlds of Adventure outside Cleveland, Ohio. The Bobs was inspired by the great classic Riverview Bobs, an early Prior and Church masterpiece in Chicago. Opened in 1988, the Raging Wolf Bobs was a rare throwback to the 1920s roller coasters, and Dinn and Summers were soon swamped with orders for rambunctious wooden roller coasters. They would not disappoint their customers.

Over the next few years, Dinn and Summers would build several coasters that today rank among the best in operation. The Timber Wolf at Kansas City, Missouri's Worlds of Fun features amazing airtime; and the Georgia

The Beast, under construction. (Courtesy of Paramount's Kings Island)

Cyclone, based on the design of the Coney Island original, is the only copy that comes close to being quite as ferocious as its namesake.

Dinn and Summers created their masterpiece at Six Flags Over Texas in 1990. The Texas Giant has consistently ranked as one of the world's best wooden roller coasters since its opening day. Wild, rambunctious and radical, the Giant has all the best elements of every great wooden coaster wrapped into one stunning package.

William Cobb and Associates

Bill Cobb had been in the business of building coasters long before he branched out on his own. He had worked closely with John Allen on some of his masterpieces, providing the structural engineering for the Great American Scream Machine in Georgia, and the Screamin' Eagle in Missouri, both for the Six Flags Company.

In 1975, Cobb was asked by Six Flags to examine the Coney Island Cyclone, which had temporarily ceased to operate. Six Falgs was thinking of purchasing the 1927 ride and moving it to its Astroworld park in Houston, Texas. Cobb determined that, although work could be done to restore the classic for operation at its present location, it would be less expensive to build a completely new ride in Houston. Six Flags received permission to copy the Cyclone, and Cobb went to work designing a larger, faster version of the older ride for the new park. When the Texas Cyclone opened in 1976, it was hailed as the world's number one roller coaster. A mirror image of the original, it had larger and slightly steeper drops.

In 1983, Cobb was asked to build another Cyclone, this time for Riverside Park in Agawam, Massachusetts (now Six Flags New England). Unfortunately, the park only had a small parcel of land to build the ride on, and it was determined that a very different ride would have to be designed. Since park owners also wanted a ride of at least 100 feet in height, Cobb had to design a roller coaster with severely steep drops and viciously tight, twisted turns. Revered by coaster fans as a true return to the masterworks of Prior and Church and Harry Traver, the Riverside Cyclone became Cobb's masterpiece. Unfortunately, after eighteen years of operation, this hard-riding monster was deemed a bit too hard-riding by new park owners Six Flags and was redesigned to remove most of its most impressive action, thereby leaving a ride that is only a shadow of its former self.

Cobb went on to build Le Monstre at La Ronde in Montreal, Canada. A dual-track racing coaster, it features a lift height of 132 feet, making it the tallest racing coaster in the world.

Cobb's assistant, John Pierce, went out on his own upon Cobb's death in

~~~~~~

Roller Coaster Fact: Bill Cobb, when questioned on the wildness of his design for the Riverside Cyclone, responded by saying, "I had gas the night before I thought that one up."

~~~~~~

1991. Pierce built four coasters before quickly retiring, the most notable being the Rattler at Six Flags Fiesta Texas in San Antonio. At 180 feet, it was the tallest wooden roller coaster in the world for many years, although its impressive 166 foot drop (one of the best ever on a wooden roller coaster) was shortened several seasons ago to a still impressive 124 feet.

Roller Coaster Corporation of America

Largely involved in the engineering of many of the early 1970s John Allen and Bill Cobb designs, RCCA branched out into building their own rides at a later date. They are responsible for the Rattler at Six Flags Fiesta Texas in San

Batman—The Ride, a great example of an inverted coaster. (Courtesy of Six Flags Great Adventure)

Antonio, the White Canyon in Japan, Montezum, South America's largest wooden coaster, in Brazil, and most recently, Son of Beast, currently the world's largest wooden coaster, at Paramount's Kings Island in Ohio.

Bolliger and Mabillard

Swiss designers and engineers Walter Bolliger and Claude Mabillard introduced their first coaster at Six Flags Great America in Illinois. Iron Wolf, a steel looping stand-up coaster, took the world by storm in 1990 because of its extreme smoothness.

In 1992, the company introduced a ride that made the entire amusement industry stand up and take notice. The inverted coaster featured ski-lift-style vehicles with trains of cars hanging below the track. The ride, also residing in Six Flags Great America, was capable of executing inversions, including several never before attempted, like heartline spins. Dubbed Batman–The Ride, the coaster was unlike anything ever created for an amusement park before. Larger versions soon appeared at Ohio's Cedar Point (Raptor) and both Busch Gardens parks, with Florida's Montu in stiff competiton with Virginia's Alpengeist for the title of best of its type.

It was a project in 1993, however, that made B&M the steel coaster manufacturer most in demand throughout the world. Kumba, also at Busch Gardens in Florida, was not a new-fangled "gimmick" roller coaster. No dangling legs, no standing passengers. Kumba was a traditional sit-down looping steel roller coaster, basically the same concept that had been in use by parks for twenty years. Its extreme smoothness, outrageous new-style inversions, and sheer quality ensure the ride a top position on any top ten list.

B&M brought the world the first "floorless" coaster in 1999. Basically taking the concept of Kumba for track layout and design, but with trains consisting of a chair directly mounted to wheels (missing floors, fronts, and sides, thereby dangling passengers' feet directly over the track), Medusa at Six Flags Great Adventure became an instant hit, and led to a building boom of large, looping coasters. The same year, B&M entered the non-looping hypercoaster market with Apollo's Chariot at Virginia's Busch Gardens. Still utilizing their own trademark four-across seating, the open air vehicles that fly through Apollo's course expose riders about as much as is safely possible, truly enhancing the feeling of flying like a bird.

Custom Coasters International

CCI is a family company, with strong roots in the coaster building business. President Denise Dinn Larris is the daughter of famed builder Charlie Dinn. Larrick's husband is vice president. Designers Larry Bill and Chad Miller create works that pay tribute to the great designers of the past, and former de-

Great Coasters International built the Wildcat at Hersheypark with coasters of the 1920s in mind. (Courtesy of Jennifer O'Rourke)

signer Dennis McNulty is responsible for producing most of the company's greatest, best-loved products.

When the company first started out, they were not interested in building the world's tallest anything for big-buck theme parks. Instead, they offered smaller, more affordable rides and marketed their product to the more intimate family-owned and -operated parks. This caused a bit of a wooden coaster building boom, as parks that found previous manufacturers too cost-prohibitive could now get exactly the type of ride they wanted, and from exactly the type of people they wanted to do business with. Since 1992, the company has built dozens of wooden coasters. They also started to get involved with the major theme parks as well, producing huge rides as well as the smaller ones they became famous for. Their mainstay now seems to be in designing rides without even the remotest dose of "finesse," producing hard-core rides that have all the design artistry of a bulldozer rampaging through a sleepy village.

Great Coasters International

Designer Mike Boodley and builder Clair Hain left CCI and formed their own company in 1995. Their first project, the Wildcat at Hersheypark in Pennsylvania, was a complete rethinking of the great rides of the 1920s. Chock-filled with Harry Traver spiral dips and Prior and Church banked turns, the Wildcat became a modern masterpiece based on classic designs, and it was an instant hit. An even stronger reverential touch came with 1999's Roar, at Six Flags Marine World, in Vallejo, California. With that ride, the company introduced its Millennium Flyer trains, single seat, articulated open-front designs that are based on the trains that Prior and Church used in the 1920s. These beautiful vehicles, because of the short wheelbase on each car, are capable of hugging the track and executing transitions better than any other coaster train in the world. They make riders feel as if they are right back in 1928. Roar itself is in the grand style of P&C's Bobs coasters, all graceful spirals and swoops. GCI outdid themselves with Hersheypark's Lightning Racer, a dual-track racing and dueling coaster, featuring moments where the

A B&M floorless coaster, Medusa, at Six Flags Great Adventure in New Jersey.. (Courtesy of Six Flags Great Adventure)

STEEL FORCE
Dorney Park

Key Facts:

Type of Design:	Out-and-back steel coaster with 360-degree spiral, tubular steel track	**Maximum Speed:**	Approximately 75 m.p.h.
		Ride Duration:	Approximately 3 minutes
Highest Points:	1st Hill: 200 Feet 2nd Hill: 161 Feet	**Number of Trains:**	3
Height of Main Drop:	205 Feet	**Capacity Per Train:**	36
Length of Track:	5,600 Feet (more than 1 mile)	**Capacity Per Hour:**	Approximately 1,700
Tunnels:	One 120-feet-long with double track running in opposite directions	**Designer:**	D.H. Morgan Manufacturing, Inc. La Selva Beach, CA

(Courtesy of Dorney Park)

two trains on opposing tracks actually split from their side-by-side course and head toward each other! GCI understands better than anyone that a ride must be artistic and dramatic and uses their talents to build the best quality (in all aspects) wooden coasters on planet Earth.

Vekoma International

A mostly steel coaster manufacturer based in the Netherlands, Vekoma has used patents held by Arrow Dynamics and ideas from B&M to create affordable production models of some of the former companies' most popular rides. Vekoma is an extremely prolific supplier of coasters, and its suspended looping model is one of the most popular coaster installations worldwide, outdone in sales only by the Boomerang, another Vekoma product that is the most widely sold production-model coaster in the world. Recently, the company has enhanced the Boomerang by providing models with below-the-track, ski-lift seating vehicles, and has also produced a substantially larger model with similar seating. Vekoma also introduced the world to the "flying" coaster, a four-across seating vehicle that passengers ride lying down, that flips to hang them below the track, enabling them to literally feel like they're flying through the looping, twisting course.

Chance/Morgan

Taking a cue from Arrow Dynamics, Morgan Manufacturing, which started in the business by making wooden coaster trains completely of fiberglass, began producing huge, non-looping steel coasters. It's first, Wild Thing, at Valleyfair! in Minnesota, was a hit due to its smoothness, and the following year, Steel Force at Dorney Park in Allentown, Pennsylvania, became known as one of the best roller coasters on Earth, because of its intensity of design and engineering craftsmanship. The company is responsible for Steel Dragon, currently the title holder of world's longest, tallest, and fastest roller coaster. At 318 feet tall and over 8,000 feet in length, the ride is capable of achieving speeds over 90 mph.

3 GETTING THE MOST WHEN YOU COAST

You might think that roller coastering is a simple endeavor. Go to the park, wait on the line, ride the ride, and move on to the next.

Well, you can certainly do it that way, and you'll probably enjoy yourself just fine. But there are shortcuts and tricks of the trades that we "professionals" have been using for years to get maximum enjoyment from our park trips.

Follow these tips and you'll get more rides, wait in line less time, and enhance your ride experience. In short, you'll enjoy riding roller coasters much more.

RAINY DAYS SHOULDN'T GET YOU DOWN

Parks are much, much less crowded when it rains, or even when it looks like rain. To avoid lines, plan to go to the parks when the sun doesn't look like it's going to be making an appearance, because the absence of the sun will also bring with it the absence of thousands of people as well. If that isn't enough, roller coasters with wet tracks run much faster than they normally do when dry. Be warned, however, that some parks do not operate coasters in even the slightest rain, and no park runs any tall ride at all when rain is accompanied by lightning. Also keep in mind that small crowds and a faster-running roller coaster are a trade-off for being soaked to the skin. And a driving rain hitting your face while you're traveling at 60 mph may not be the most pleasurable thing you'll ever experience.

IT DOES MATTER WHERE YOU SIT—AND HOW!

Most parks let you sit in whatever seat you choose to on a roller coaster. In these cases, the front and back seats will always have longer lines than any other seat. Contrary to what some people will tell you, it does matter where

The Great American Scream Machine. (Courtesy of Six Flags Great Adventure)

you sit. Certain rides are better in the front; others, in back. Generally, a roller coaster is smoother in the front, and much snappier in the back. The middle of the train neutralizes the extremes felt at either end, offering not much more than a fast trip along the track.

The front of a roller coaster train tends to "hang" down the drops, as it is being held back by the rear of the train. However, it is pushed quite severely up the hills and through inversions, enabling passengers to feel more extreme forces of gravity. If you require an unobstructed view of the track, sit in the front seat (Seat number two will not even come close to providing the same visual, so don't settle for it if the front-seat line is too long). If your reason for sitting in the front is to experience the extreme g-forces, as well as negative g's (those delicious moments where your body lifts off the seat and you become weightless), only sit in the front if there's no line. While the negative g's are fine in the front seat, they are even more accentuated in the third seat (this applies only to non-looping wood and steel coasters).

The back of a train will be yanked down each drop, enabling those sitting in the rear to experience the full force and length of the drop. (This is the effect that causes some people to think the back of the train "goes faster" than the front, which is impossible, of course—the back of a coaster train has never been known to return to the station before the front of the train!) Passengers in the rear, depending on the severity of the design, tend to be catapulted out of the seat on the drop, making the ride generally much wilder than in any other place on the train. The back seat is the most severe, but if the line is too long, the one right in front of it is usually almost as good.

Wherever you choose to sit—front, back, or middle—whether or not you sit directly over the wheels also determines the nature of your ride. Each coaster train is usually comprised of from three to seven cars. Each car will either have two seats (seating four passengers total) or three seats (seating six). Each individual car has four wheels, two in front and two in back, which ride above the rails and enable the train to roll forward. Sitting in the rear seat of the car (third on three-bench cars, scond on two-bench) will result in a rougher ride. Not only are you directly above the wheels that are making contact with the track, there is nothing solid behind your seat to act as a shock absorber (additional cars linked to the rear of your car will not serve this purpose). If that's what you want, have at it. But if you're looking for a smoother ride, choose the seat over the front wheels, or in the case of three-bench cars, the middle seat, which is not over wheels at all. Your teeth won't rattle, but you'll still feel all the gravity forces.

Wherever you sit, how you sit will also affect your ride. If you like to hold your hands in the air, go right ahead. Keep in mind, though, that holding your arms up forces you to stiffen your body somewhat; this may make you fight against the natural flow of the ride. Try sitting with your body relaxed (for some, this won't be an easy thing to do). Let your hands rest on the lap-bar, or hold on lightly. You'll really get the experience of whatever ride you're on.

TO SEE OR NOT TO SEE

If you're afraid—whatever you do, DO NOT CLOSE YOUR EYES!!! What you can't see is much scarier than what you can see, and riding a roller coaster with your eyes closed will only make the experience all the more terrifying. (This also works in reverse for serious thrill seekers. If you want to make the ride more frightening, just close your eyes!) You won't be able to see the hills, twists, or loops coming, and your body won't be able to register what's happening until it's too late. Not being able to anticipate is what makes even the most mild indoor-in-the-dark or backward coaster so intense.

Roller Coaster Fact: Among the lost items found beneath roller coasters—in addition to the expected wallets, loose change, and keys—have been several rather mysterious curiosities such as a glass eye, a prosthetic leg, brassieres, and more false teeth than could possibly be imagined. Strangely enough, many of these items remain unclaimed by their owners.

FACING BACKWARD

Some parks have coasters that feature trains facing backward on the track. All steel shuttle loop coasters must traverse the course backward to return to their station starting points, but there are also wooden racing coasters that have one side forward, one backward. Going backward, you'll experience all the forces that are part of the forward coastering experieince, but you will feel them quite differently. (An example: forward inertia will push the rider back into his seat going forward—backward, that same rider will be pushed away from the seat.) Keep in mind that since none of the course will be visible to you, a backward ride will be more physical and somewhat scarier, as we just discussed above.

WHAT DO I RIDE FIRST?

Try to arrive at the park just before the gates open. If you're not familiar with the park's layout, get a map (either handed to you at the parking tool booth, or available at the main entrance ticket booth). Take a few minutes to find the roller coasters you want to ride. When the gates open, unless you really must ride the roller coaster nearest the front gate, head for the coaster that is furthest away. Most people go immediately to whatever major attraction is closest, so you'll have at least a few rides without any lines before others start to show up. By afternoon, you'll find the shortest lines of the day on those rides close to the entrance, as by that tiime the crowds will have moved further into the park. You'll also find that just before park closing, rides further from the front gate will have the shortest lines.

When a park opens a new roller coaster, or any big, splashy new attraction, by all means go to the park. If you can wait to ride the new ride until a later date, you just might find yourself with no lines to wait on at all for anything else. Almost everyone will be queued up to ride the new attraction.

Always check to see how many trains are running on a roller coaster before you wait in line. If the particular coaster you want to ride is only running one train, check back later. A long line with a two or three trains running moves much swifter than a shorter line with only one train. Of course, if there's no line at all, it doesn't matter.

Some pay-one-price parks allow you to reride without exiting and reentering the line. This happens only when there is no line, and no one is waiting for your seat. Since people will always queue up for the front or back seats, sitting nearer the middle of the train will probably ensure you more rides without having to get off the train and walk around. If the park does not offer this policy, you'll have no choice but to exit at the end of your ride; the attendants didn't make the rules, and therefore cannot bend them.

Call the park to find out if any large group outings are scheduled for the day of your visit. (You can usually get this information several days in advance). Large groups may mean thousands of children, and most of them love roller coasters and will be standing on "your" line.

ATTENTION COASTERING PARENTS WITH SMALL CHILDREN

The minimum height restriction on adult coasters usually ranges from 42 to 54 inches, which prohibits most young children from riding. These height restrictions are determined by the type of restraints contained in the vehicle, as well as the nature of the ride itself. They are always strictly enforced.

Many parks have child-size roller coasters that allow adults to ride if accompanied by kids. Most parks also offer a "parent swap" program for couples and families who wish to ride an adult coaster but do not have nonriding adults to leave the children with. One adult rides the coaster while the other waits at the exit of the ride with the kids. When the first adult has ridden, he or she switches places with the one who first stayed with the little ones, affording both adults a ride without waiting in line two separate times. This policy is typically not made widely known, and the logistics may vary from park to park, so check with Guest Services regarding the exact policy in effect at the park before you attempt to ride in this manner.

HANDICAPPED POLICIES

Most parks offer special services for physically challenged guests. These days, amsuement rides are all generally wheelchair accessible, and available to most guests, depending on what the individual's disability may be. Don't attempt to ride before you've checked on what rules and regulations may be in effect at the park you're visiting, and what the particular ride's requirements might be. You can get this information at Guest Services.

THEME PARKS CAN BE EXPENSIVE . . .

. . . unless you play your cards right. Try to buy your tickets in advance through AAA or other sources. There's usually a small discount.

Some parks offer two day tickets at considerable savings. Coupons are also frequently available throughout areas local to the particular park, in fast food venues, or supermarkets. If you plan on visiting a park more than twice in a season, your best bet would be to purchase a season pass. Season passes often sell for a price less than the amount it would cost to visit the park in question twice. Additionally, season pass holders are often invited to exclusive parties at the park, and may receive discount coupons good for free visits, discounted merchandise, etc.

Several theme park companies now also offer the option of using a season pass purchased at one park in all other parks they own and operate, for free admission. A Six Flags pass purchased at any Six Flags park is good for use at all Six Flags Theme Parks and Theme Park Properties (except for the water parks within the chain). Paramount Parks offers the same deal. Cedar Fair, LP, owns six parks (Cedar Point, Sandusky, Ohio; Valleyfair!, Shakopee, Minnesota; Dorney Park and Wildwater Kingdom, Allentown, Pennsylvania; Worlds of Fun/Oceans of Fun, Kansas City, Missouri; Knott's Berry Farm, Buena Park, California; and Michigan's Adventure, Muskegon, Michigan) and allows admission to all of them with one park's season pass. Note, however, that the policy usually does not include parking fees, and you must have a processed pass from the park you purchased it in to enter the other parks.

Busch Gardens does not currently offer free admission to holders of season passes from its other parks within the chain, but does offer certain discounts on parking and merchandise.

OBSERVE ALL RULES OF THE GAME

Do not attempt to stand up when riding, or engage in any other unsafe activities. If you do, the park will eject you from its property, at the very least. You might find yourself in even more hot water, as in some places it is a misdemeanor crime to engage in unsafe practices on amusement devices. Of course, the worst possible outcome—that you or others could be hurt or killed—in itself should be the key reason to abide by all riding rules. If you feel that the roller coaster isn't thrilling enough unless you attempt to stand up or commit other foolish acts, then maybe coaster riding isn't for you, and you need to find something else to do with your time.

4 TYPES OF ROLLER COASTERS

Roller coasters come in all different shapes, sizes and varieties. In this chapter, you can familiarize yourself with the different types of rides you'll be encountering in subsequent pages, as well as on trips to the actual parks.

WOOD

Wooden roller coasters have been operating in the United States since 1884. Not much has changed in ensuing years—the ride is still a somewhat simple concept, and doesn't offer any high-tech variations at all. Yet purists will tell you wood is what roller coastering is all about. While steel coasters come in many different varieties, there are just two wood variations. The reason for this is either because steel is capable of more acrobatics, or because wood is capable of accomplishing its goals without the gimmicks that steel relies on.

While some wood coasters are dual-tracked racing versions and some feature trains facing backward on the track, the two major different types of wood coasters are as follows:

• *Twister* The track is all twisted and tied up in knots, like spaghetti in a bowl, featuring criss-crossing trackage, many turns, and steep drops. Fans of wooden twisters point out that this type of ride offers more surprises than out and backs, with hidden drops and sudden turns.

• *Out and back* Very simple in layout, basically starting out at point A, moving to point B, and returning to point A. Dual-track racing coasters are commnly designed as out and backs. A variation on the standard out and back is the double out and back, which moves from A to B, back to A, then back to B, and finishes at A.

Roar, Six Flags Marine World with Millennium Flyer trains that brings the 1920s coaster riding experience into the 21st century. (Courtesy of Great Coasters International)

Roller Coaster Fact: The Viper at Six Flags Magic Mountain in Valencia, California, at 188 feet, is the world's tallest looping steel roller coaster, although the Steel Phantom at Kennywood (near Pittsburgh, Pennsylvania), with a drop of 225 feet down a mountainside, offers the longest steel looping drop and the fastest speed..

STEEL

• *Looping* Any standard (trains riding above the track, with passengers sitting in a normal position) roller coaster that goes upside down.

• *Non-looping* Usually large, standard rides that do not feature any upside-down elements.

• *Inverted* Looping coaster with trains hanging below the track. Passengers sit in ski-lift-type vehicles, their legs dangling below them in the open air.

• *Suspended* Non-looping ride with enclosed trains hanging below the track. Suspended coaster trains swing freely with each turn, while inverted coaster trains are locked and fixed to the track.

• *Stand-up* A coaster with vehicles designed to accommodate passengers in a standing, upright position; usually looping.

• *Floorless* A standard looping coaster, but with vehicles that have been stripped down of all surrounding sideboards and floor, leaving what amounts to a kitchen chair that is directly attached to wheels.

• *Flying Coaster* Featuring vehicles in which riders are lying down, face down, much of the time.

• *Mine Train* Family-type themed ride, with trains resembling locomotives or mining cars. Mine trains are big on small drops and lots of twists and turns.

Steel Force, Dorney Park (in background, looming over little wooden brother Thunder Hawk). (Author's collection)

• *Bobsled* Single cars or trains running freely inside a trough, just like a real boblsed.

• *Shuttle* Any coaster that returns backward along the same track, whether in a straight line or in a course with many twists and turns. Shuttles usually have inversions, but don't necessarily have to contain them.

• *Compact Portable* Any type of small, traveling roller coaster, commonly with cars for one, two or four passengers. Many parks offer such rides as permanent attractions, even though they can be easily moved.

There are also several variations of roller coasters that can be constructed of wood or steel:

• *Terrain* Rides that use the topography of the earth to dictate their layouts and profiles. Found in parks with hills, ravines, mountains, etc.

• *Junior* Rides that are not quite as large as their adult, full-size versions, but not necessarily small enough to be considered strictly for children. Not to be confused with steel compact portables, although they are often similar in size.

• *Kiddie* Small coasters designed for children, although adults are frequently welcome to ride, if they can fit into the child-size cars.

5 THE WORLD'S BEST WOOD COASTERS

THE ULTIMATE WOOD COASTER

CYCLONE

Coney Island's Astroland, Brooklyn, New York

An unequaled achievement in the combination of sharp drops and tight turns, the most famous roller coaster in the world (and a National Historic Landmark) is still considered to be the best wood ride there is. In a time when mega-monsters are being built, the 85-foot-tall first drop still sends shock waves of fright through riders, and this may be the only roller coaster in history to have appeared on nearly every coaster top ten list ever produced. Built in 1927 at the height of the early coaster wars, this masterpiece was crammed into a space that had previously been home to the world's first roller coaster, and the world's first looping roller coaster, causing a pronounced "sharpness" to its drops and turns that simply does not exist on any roller coaster built today. Just prior to the 1998 season, a restoration project began on the ride (which is still ongoing) to restore it to its 1927 operating condition, which increased its speed, smoothness, and, ultimately, its thrills.

~~~~~~

Roller Coaster Fact: The oldest wooden roller coaster in operation is Leap the Dips at Lakemont Park, Altoona, Pennsylvania, dating back to 1904 and still in its original location. The oldest steel coaster is Disneyland's Matterhorn, which opened in 1959.

~~~~~~

Texas Giant at Six Flags Over Texas. (Courtesy of Bobby Nagy)

FIVE STAR WOOD COASTERS

BOSS

Six Flags St. Louis, Allenton, Missouri

A way huge ride built on a mountainside, utilizing terrain to provide some hair-raising drops throughout the course. A terrifying double dip comprises the first drop, followed by an ingenious layout that includes large drops, rabbit hops, and a helix finale—a truly intense ride.

BOULDER DASH

Lake Compounce, Bristol, Connecticut

This very long roller coaster features the best and most abundant airtime to be found on any wooden roller coaster in the world. Built on the side of a mountain, the constantly twisting and turning layout dodges trees, boulders (hence, it's name), and provides a truly exhilarating experience. What it lacks in good drops it makes up for in sheer action.

Roller Coaster Fact: The late Ruth Voss, for many years director of public relations at what is now known as Paramount's Kings Island, was afflicted with arthritis. She found that a ride on the Beast each morning "loosened her up" and alleviated much of the stiffness associated with the disease.

COMET

The Great Escape, Lake George, New York

This 96-foot-high ride originally opened at Crystal Beach Park, on the Canadian shores of Lake Erie near Buffalo, New York. When that park closed in 1989, the ride was purchased and moved to this park, now a member of the Six Flags chain. Reopened in 1994, the rebuilt and restored Comet proved to be an even better coaster than it was in its original home. A double out and back design, it features huge hills and a constant speed providing tremendous moments of airtime. The Comet is 4,000 feet of total, wild abandonment.

CYCLONE

Six Flags New England, Agawam, Massachusetts

Another coaster inspired by 1920s classics—in this case, however, no single design, but insane elements indictive of the style most prevalent during that time—and exaggerated in concept to boot. The park wanted a ride of a certain height, but only had a small parcel of land available to build on, so designer Bill Cobb was forced to make each drop treacherously steep and the turns truly wicked. The ride's crowning glory, a first drop consisting of an awesome 200-degree turn during a supersteep double dip, was redesigned in 2001 to remove much of its severity.

GEORGIA CYCLONE

Six Flags Over Georgia, Atlanta, Georgia

In the mid-1970s, the Six Flags family of theme parks wanted to purchase the original Coney Island Cyclone and move it to Six Flags Astroworld in Houston, Texas. For financial reasons, they decided to ask permission to build a replica instead. The result was the Texas Cyclone, a larger, faster, and wilder version of the original. A full fourteen years later, and after much taming of the Houston copy, the company built its second Cyclone at its Georgia facility. Two others followed in other Six Flags parks. None of the copies come close to the level of intensity of the Brooklyn one-and-only, but this southern version approaches the wildness of its namesake. Judged on its own merits, the Georgia Cyclone is one of the best kick-butt roller coasters on the planet. Its "slammer" qualities on each of its steep hills are among the best in the business.

GHOST RIDER

Knott's Berry Farm, Buena Park, California

A huge, L-shaped twister with a hidden helix along the way, this ride is all about speed, hills, changes of direction, and relentless pacing. The first drop, which dives into the ride's structure and takes a left turn at the bottom, is only the beginning of a roller coaster that never lets up. Ghost Rider was an immediate hit with coaster fans and park guests, and remains the number one ride at one of the nation's most popular theme parks.

GRIZZLY

Paramount's Kings Dominion, Doswell, Virginia

This has got to be one of the sneakiest roller coasters in the world. It was completely hidden in the woods until just a few seasons ago, when the park begin clearing land for expansion purposes. Approaching it from the parks' entrance still leaves this ride shrouded in mystery, however, and even from the station not much can be detected. Once you are on the ride, there's still trickery afoot. Grizzly's first drop, a twisting 85-footer, is comparatively mild, and immediately following that, the ride has an extremely slow, flat turn. At this moment, most passengers are thinking how they just wasted forty-five minutes in line, but then "Grizz" shifts into overdrive, becoming of the wildest, most action-packed rides around. Along the way, passengers are treated to a hidden tunnel that, most assuredly, appears too small for the train to fit into. Based on a defunct 1920s classic, Grizzly is perhaps the greatest use of psychology in roller coaster design.

LEGEND

Holiday World, Santa Claus, Indiana

When this park built the Raven in the mid-1990s, it was an instant hit—and the park wisely followed up by building an appropriately named ride that was similar in style and concept to that ride, but bigger, longer, steeper, and just more, more, more. Legend features tunnels, utilizes terrain for hidden drops, and may just be unequaled in the world in non-stop pacing and action. The *best* terrain coaster in the world.

LIGHTNING RACER

Hersheypark, Hershey, Pennsylvania

A true beauty, with a dueling, racing layout which features trains not only racing side by side, but also has changes in the twin-track layout that have the trains heading for each other! At one point in the course, the tracks actually dive over and under each other, thereby making the opposing train not only be at your side or hurtling towards you, but also flying over your head and immediately diving under you. A true masterpiece of artistic design.

PHOENIX

Knoebel's Amusement Resort, Elysburg, Pennsylvania

A true fan favorite, this might be one of the most perfect little rides in the world. Not of great size, the Phoenix has respectable hills, but it truly hits its stride in a series of rabbit hops perfectly designed to produce airtime.

RAMPAGE

Visionland, Alabama

The design of this ride features a large drop into a wild series of choppy hills, sharp twists, and turns that contain nasty laterals in a compact course that will leave riders breathless.

RAVEN

Holiday World, Santa Claus, Indiana

While this little terror might be a bit short, what it does during its circuit always leaves riders cheering. A good sized drop into a tunnel is followed by airtime-producing hills and sharp turns. At its midpoint, things really get going, as the track takes a long dive into a valley, and stays flat, dodging trees and following the terrain. Wild direction changes make up the last few seconds.

ROAR

Six Flags Marine World, Vallejo, California

This roller coaster is a tribute to the great designs of Prior and Church, builders of some of the most graceful and thrilling coasters of the 1920s. What really makes this creation of spiral drops and unforseen direction changes, however, are its trains. They are design replicas of Prior and Church vehicles, consisting of single-seat, open-front cars linked together. The cars not only snake along the track beautifully, but also are able to take sharp turns and drops with utmost grace. Definitely one of the best rides, and ride experiences, there is.

SHIVERING TIMBERS

Michigan's Adventure, Muskegon, Michigan

This is one of those coasters that can only be described as "epic in proportion." At 125 feet, it is very large for a coaster made entirely of wood. Its out-and-back design consists of a series of huge camelbacks on the way out, a large turn-around, and smaller, air producing rabbit hops on the way back, with a tight-radius helix at the finish. The design of this ride is so classic, there should be a photograph of it in the dictionary next to the definition of roller coaster.

TEXAS GIANT

Six Flags Over Texas, Arlington, Texas

This masterpiece of mayhem has a 143-foot-tall lift-hill that leads riders into an absolute maelstrom of twists and dives that are nearly unequaled by any other amusement device, wood, steel, or otherwise. In the years since this ultimate ride came on the scene, sections of it that were deemed a little too intense have been redesigned. Still, this bucking bronco, although somewhat tamer, but markedly faster, remains without peer. In fact, each year, it becomes an even more fine-tuned terror inducer.

TWISTER

Knoebel's Amusement Resort, Elysburg, Pennsylvania

Based on the design of a much-loved favorite of the same name in the old Elitch Gardens in Denver, this amazing ride packs about as much punch as a coaster can. Right out of the gate, passengers know they're experiencing something special when they encounter the first lift-hill, which is located directly under the second (space constraints dictated that the lift-hill be split in this way to bring the ride to its full height). The drops and turns that follow are truly beautifully designed, with just the right pitch, and when the trains roar into the double helix that gives this ride its name, you just know that you're in the eye of the storm. It's a masterpiece, and the few changes made in the design from the original actually have improved the experience.

WHITE CYCLONE

Nagashima Spaland, Mei-ken, Japan

A huge, extremely fast ride with two reverse-direction helices, large drops, rabbit hops, all combined with exquisite pacing and strong dramatic sensibility. Only the second wooden roller coaster ever built in Japan

WILDCAT

Hersheypark, Hershey, Pennsylvania

One of the first rides to harken back to the designs of 1920 masters Prior and Church, featuring a series of beautiful spiral drops that lead to constant changes of direction. This is a fun, exciting, and very nostalgic ride.

Roller Coaster Fact: The Coney Island Cyclone, although a wooden roller coaster, has a mostly steel structure, because local ordinances prohibited the building of wood structures beyond a certain height.

6 THE WORLD'S BEST STEEL ROLLER COASTERS

ULTIMATE STEEL COASTER

SUPERMAN RIDE OF STEEL

Six Flags New England, Agawam, Massachusetts

It's really difficult to name this ride simply as the best steel roller coaster in the world because there is nothing, wood or steel, that comes close to providing the type of experience that this masterpiece does. It may just be the best coaster on planet Earth. A non-looping hypercoaster from Intamin, and an extreme machine bar none, SROS begins with a heartpounding 221-foot-long drop at over 70 degrees that dives into an underground tunnel that is impossibly long, dark, and fog-filled. Rocketing out of this abyss, the train flies over hills that produce airtime galore, and takes a turn that is overbanked (virtually upside down). A diabolical figure-eight section wrings sweat out of riders, and a second foggy tunnel comes out of the blue to hit them squarely between the eyes. *Then,* a finale of sharp rabbit hops totally blitzes the rider into submission, and the sudden stop just outside the station leaves them screaming long after all motion has stopped. There may be some truly great coasters out there, but this one leads the pack, and all the others have to eat a bit of its dust.

~~~~~~

Roller Coaster Fact: Six Flags New England's Thunderbolt was based on plans from the Cyclone, a wooden roller coaster that operated at the Flushing, New York, World's Fair in 1939.

~~~~~~

FIVE STAR STEEL COASTERS

ALPENGEIST

Busch Gardens, Williamsburg, Virginia

It's one of the most terrifying roller coasters currently in operation, largely because of its enormous size. It's an inverted coaster, with chair-lift style vehicles hanging below the track, which enhance the passenger's sense of flying. This mountain ghost is 195-feet tall, with a 17-story first drop, absolutely huge looping elements, and amazing speed. The ride is built at the edge of a ravine, into which it travels deeper and deeper with each inversion. For its grand finale, Alpengeist treats passengers to a few ground-hugging moments where it would be best if riders were not wearing platform shoes!

BATMAN AND ROBIN–THE CHILLER

Six Flags Great Adventure, Jackson, New Jersey

Not one, but two different track profiles, in a similar basic layout, this linear induction motor launch shuttle catapults riders from 0-70 mph in 4 seconds, flips them through inversions (two on Batman, three on Robin), and soars them up a 200-foot tower, at which time the train rockets backward through the same course. The train was retrofitted with lap-bars only in 2001-2002, making the experience of flying with total freedom and smoothness quite exceptional, and truly making this ride one of the most intense, if not *the* most intense, coaster on the planet.

BATMAN KNIGHT FLIGHT

Six Flags Worlds of Adventure, Aurora, Ohio

A Bolliger and Mabillard floorless coaster with a few extreme moments that do not involve inversions, but missing the zero-g roll that is probably B&M's best inversion element.

~~~~~~

Roller Coaster Fact: Batman–The Ride at Six Flags Great America (Illinois) was the first roller coaster ever built that required special rules regarding riders' shoes.

~~~~~~

BATMAN–THE RIDE

Six Flags Theme Parks, (Illinois, New Jersey, California, Missouri, Texas, Georgia)

The amusement industry was rocked off its foundation in 1992, when B&M debuted its first inverted roller coaster, Batman–The Ride, at Six Flags Great America. The ride caused a sensation among parkgoers as well, and while other parks clamored to sign contracts for their own versions, Six Flags began adding replicas to each of it's own parks. Themed to the long-popular Batman character, and specifically to the recent Batman motion picture series, the rides are identical in layout (except for the St. Louis version, which is a mirror image), although the theming varies from park to park.

EXPEDITION GEFORCE

Hansa Park, Neustadt-Holstein, Germany

This is a non-looper with a huge twisting first drop leading to a spaghetti bowl of hills, turns, and twists, from the masters of roller coaster thrills, Intamin, currently the builders of the best non-looping hypercoasters in the world. This version, instead of following the traditional out-and-back course that most hypers take, is a twister, in the truest sense of the word, with a track layout almost impossible to follow, and strategically hidden by the park's natural landscape.

KUMBA

Busch Gardens, Tampa, Florida

This was truly the ride that cemented B&M's position as the number one steel coaster manufacturer in the world. While the company established itself developing the inverted coaster and perfecting the stand-up coaster, Kumba was their first attempt at a type of ride that had been around for years: a standard, sit-down, above-the-track looping steel roller coaster. The ride is beyond smooth and features inversion elements that the "other" guys wouldn't have even attempted to try. Riders are always stunned when, as the Kumba train is about to enter its fourth huge inversion, the train seems to pick up even more speed than it displayed previously. An absolute masterpiece.

MAGNUM XL-200

Cedar Point, Sandusky, Ohio

Magnum is of historic importance, as this was the first full-circuit roller coaster to top 200 feet in height (205 to be exact). It's also noteworthy because it doesn't go upside down even once, although it was built at a time when all other parks were racing each other to construct giant steel coasters with more loops than their competition. Magnum offered a more traditional experience, although of the giant-size variety, and set a trend in the industry to build rides that relied on the tried-and-true ups and downs of roller coasters. It's a legend, and to this day, remains one of the all time greats!

MEDUSA

Six Flags Great Adventure, Jackson, New Jersey

B&M, innovators of the steel coaster world, brought us this masterpiece, the world's first floorless coaster. While the design layout is that of a traditional huge, looping ride, the trains are similar to kitchen chairs with wheels that are locked onto the track. There is no way a rider won't think his feet are going to hit the track in front of him, and the absolute best sense of floating on track is achieved by securing a front row seat. It's smooth beyond compare, fast, and thrilling.

MEDUSA

Six Flags Marine World, Vallejo, California

Six Flags, famous for reproducing exact replicas of it's more popular rides, took a bit of a course change with this ride, a second-generation floorless that only shares a name with it's East Coast sister. The layout here is entirely new, with a new inversion element known as Sea Serpent that flips riders twice and resembles a giant bow tie. What is really awesome here is the finale, which is a series of left flips that make riders feel as if they are being drilled into the ground, all followed by a surprise right turning helix.

MILLENNIUM FORCE

Cedar Point, Sandusky, Ohio

It's no surprise that the park that brought the world the first full circuit coaster to top 200 feet should also be the park to conquer 300 feet, and this ride, which debuted in 2000, is the one that will be remembered in the history books for doing just that. Millennium Force is another non-looping steel machine, with a 310 foot height and drop that is 80 degrees steep (nearly straight down). A speed of 92 mph takes riders over hills that are designed for speed rather than severe action, which is fine as riders hurtle through the course without time to think about where they're going or even when they're going to arrive. A *great* riding experience for all.

MIND BENDER

Six Flags Over Georgia, Atlanta, Georgia

While all the other rides on this list were built from the late 1980s through now, Mind Bender came on the scene in 1978, making it an antique of sorts. This old-timer, however, is far from ready for retirement. Designed by Anton Schwarzkopf, considered to be the father of the steel roller coaster, this ride is so precisely designed and so perfectly engineered that passengers tackle its two inversion elements without the need for over-the-shoulder harnesses. A simple lap-bar is all you get on this classic, and it's all you need, as gravity holds you firmly in place at all times. Combining the loops of modern coasters with the traditional hills of an old-fashioned woodie, there's nothing quite like Mind Bender—long may she roll!

Nitro, the tallest coaster in the eastern U.S.A.. (Courtesy of Six Flags Great Adventure)

MONTU

Busch Gardens, Tampa, Florida

Although all previous inverted coasters caused sensations, this one took the best features of each and rolled them all into one: lightning quick pacing like Batman–The Ride; the original inverted (Six Flags theme Parks' signature ride); huge size (150-feet tall) like Raptor at Cedar Point; and underground tunnels like those featured on Nemesis, located at Alton Towers in England. The g-forces experienced on Montu may be among the highest that extreme roller coaster riding will permit.

NITRO

Six Flags Great Adventure, Jackson, New Jersey

B&M's entry into the non-looping hypercoaster market produced some surprisingly mild rides that were disappointments at best. Nitro, in the hard-to-please New York–East Coast market, had to do a bit more, and B&M rose admirably to the occasion by producing probably their most kick-butt ride since they got into the business. An extreme first drop, sharp hills, tight turns, and a super-small helix, all of which produce airtime, makes this one of the best coaster experiences in the world. The design is so exceptional, one can even overlook the four-across seating, which somehow, until now, didn't seem right on a roller coaster that didn't go upside down, therefore trying to recreate a traditional coaster sensation.

RAPTOR

Cedar Point, Sandusky, Ohio

B&M strikes again with this large inverted coaster. Raptor's best features come from having to be designed around existing structures on the park's midway, so that strange little twists and what can best be described as "lane changes" constantly fake out the passenger. Raptor's finest moment comes right at the beginning, with a first drop laid out as an elongated S-turn, heading into a sudden drop-off (which is best experienced in the back row on the right side) that provides the finest sense of free-fall on mostly any currently operating roller coaster.

STEEL DRAGON

Nagashima Spaland, Japan

It can only be said that this ride was built to be the tallest and longest ride in the world, which it certainly is. At 318 feet, with over 8,000 feet of track, it is hard to imagine anything soon that will beat it. That said, and taking nothing away from the ride, the design here is very similar to Magnum and particularly Steel Force, just with another 100 feet added to the top of the lift-hill. While that might not be a bad thing (actually, it most surely isn't!), when riding Steel Dragon, you might sense a bit of déjà vu.

STEEL FORCE

Dorney Park, Allentown, Pennsylvania

While it may share design similarities to older brother Magnum XL 200 (at sister park Cedar Point), much more pronounced engineering produced a more fine-tuned riding experience. Magnum is rambunctious and unperfect, while Steel Force is a bit more refined, and both rides produce similar thrills. A great first drop into a tiny underground tunnel is only the beginning of Steel Force, which runs the entire length of the park and travels within feet of both of the parks wooden roller coasters.

SUPERMAN RIDE OF STEEL

*Six Flags America, Largo, Maryland; Six Flags Darien Lake,
Buffalo, New York*

The Six Flags America ride is a mirror image of the Six Flags Darien Lake ride, which came first, and was Intamin's first entry into the non-looping hyper market. The ride caused a sensation with its very open seating, steep first drop, wicked turns, and extreme airtime producing rabbit hops. Non-stop speed is also one of the highlights of these two beauties.

TEXAS TORNADO

Astroworld, Houston, Texas

An Anton Schwarzkopf compact masterpiece of intensity, with impossibly steep drops, real roller coaster turns and hills, and four loops that leave riders feeling as if they've been through a blender.

7 THE PARKS WITH THE BEST COLLECTION OF COASTERS

THE ULTIMATE COASTER PARK

CEDAR POINT

Sandusky, Ohio

When it comes to roller coasters, this park doesn't fool around. It has fifteen of them, the most of any park iin the world. But it's not just the number of coasters that should make this park any roller coaster lover's ultimate destination. The park also has the distinction of featuring at least one of almost every variety of coaster, and some of those in operation were the longest, tallest, and fastest of their kind when first opened (and in some cases, still are).

Most important, all the coasters at Cedar Point are not what might be considered total thrill machines, and that makes this collection especially perfect for family members who might not all share the same threshold for thrills. Not everyone has the desire to dive 300 feet down at 92 mph, so the Point offers rides for those folks, too. In fact, a small child beginning his or her coaster-riding life at Cedar Point could start out on the park's kiddie coaster and "graduate" to the next level each year as height or bravery allows.

Roller Coaster Fact: Gemini, at Cedar Point in Ohio, has the highest passenger capacity of any roller coaster in the world. With two tracks running three trains each, the ride can thrill 3,000 riders per hour.

Eight (count 'em, eight!) of Cedar Point's twelve roller coasters are visible in the bird's-eye view of the world's roller coaster capital. (Courtesy of Dan Feicht)

Cedar Point has the distinction of being the only park in the world with three roller coasters that are over 200 feet tall—Magnum XL 200, (205 feet), Millennium Force, (310 feet) and Wicked Twister (215 feet).

THE TOP COASTER PARKS

BLACKPOOL PLEASURE BEACH

Blackpool, England

Four classic wooden roller coasters, along with one of the tallest steel rides in the world, are the major attractions at this ten-coaster park, a hundred-year-old British institution. Ironically, this is one of the few places left in the world where you can have a good old-fashioned *American* amusement park experience.

~~~~~~

Roller Coaster Fact: Paramount's Kings Dominion, north of Richmond, Virginia, and Blackpool Pleasure Beach, Blackpool, England, tie for having the most wooden roller coasters—four each, although Blackpool also has a wooden-tracked Wild Mouse.

~~~~~~

NAGASHIMA SPALAND

Mei-ken, Japan

There are eight coasters scattered about this amusement resort, including the top rated White Cyclone woodie, and the hard to miss Steel Dragon, currently the world's tallest, longest, and fastest roller coaster.

PARAMOUNT'S KINGS DOMINION

Doswell, Virginia

This wonderful park has the distinction of containing the most wooden roller coasters of any park in North America, a total of four, and also contains the most launching coasters as well (a whopping three). While this might seem to some redundant, all the rides here are of such differing natures, that you'll never even notice what's missing, you'll be too busy enjoying what the park does have!

PARAMOUNT'S KINGS ISLAND

Cincinnati, Ohio

This is the park familiar to fans of early *Brady Bunch* episodes. The racing coaster that Mike, Carol, and the kids rode back in 1973 has been joined by ten others in the ensuing years. In fact, the Racer is widely credited as being the roller coaster that began a renaissance of sorts for coasters; after it opened, parks began building big wooden coasters in numbers that hadn't been seen since the 1920s. The collection today offers thrills, family adventures, and several one-of-a-kind experiences, including The Beast, still the world's longest wooden coaster, and Son of Beast, the world's only looping woodie.

SIX FLAGS GREAT ADVENTURE

Jackson, New Jersey

This park is home to what might be the most thrilling collection of steel coasters in the world. The Park's Batman and Robin–The Chiller is without a doubt, number one with a bullet in the intensity department, and among the other twelve different tracks offered, there are at least four that can be described as high-thrill machines. The park is easily the thrill-ride capital of the world.

SIX FLAGS MAGIC MOUNTAIN

Valencia, California

Six Flags is the largest operator of parks and roller coasters in the world. Fifteen rides alone reside in this Southern California location. This collection tends to be more thrill-ride oriented, but families will find a few suitable to their level as well. The variety and quality of the coasters here establish Six Flags Magic Mountain as the park with the best collection of thrilling rides in the western United States.

SIX FLAGS OVER GEORGIA

Atlanta, Georgia

This nine ride collection of roller coasters is a rather straightforward bunch, with not as much unusual high-tech gimmickry available. The offerings here are, for the most part, more traditional up and down—or up, upside down, and down—but what distinguishes these rides is their sheer abundance of quality. Two wooden rides are among the best of their type, and two of the steelies are also top ten material. All of the roller coasters at this park are of the thrill variety, even the park's runaway mine train, often the type of ride designed exclusively for the family trade. Those in search of kick-ass roller coasters will love this park.

SIX FLAGS OVER TEXAS

Arlington, Texas

Like Six Flags Over Georgia, this grouping of coasters is of the more traditional kind, and of great quality. What sets it apart is that it offers several family-type rides, as well as just about every conceivable type of ride currently available.

SIX FLAGS WORLDS OF ADVENTURE

Aurora, Ohio

A classic park known as Geauga Lake, which was bought by Six Flags and transformed into this huge facility, is jam-packed with coasters, both old and new. Joining the 1920s Big Dipper woodie are a floorless, an inverted, two other more modern woodies, and probably a lot more to come.

Roller Coaster Fact: The steepest drops on roller coasters have rarely been more than 60 degrees, until the 1997 debut of Batman and Robin—The Chiller at Six Flags Great Adventure (Jackson, New Jersey) and Mr. Freeze at both Six Flags Over Texas (Arlington, Texas) and Six Flags St. Louis (Allenton, Missouri). All three feature 90-degree drops from a height of well over 100 feet—that's straight down, folks!

8 THE GUIDE TO ROLLER COASTERS WORLDWIDE

The guide to roller coasters worldwide lists all operating wooden roller coasters and most steel. Each listing includes the name of the ride, whether it is made of wood or steel, the type of coaster it is, and a rating, plus any comments about the ride that may be of interest.

The two-part rating system is exclusive to *The Roller Coaster Lover's Companion*. The first rating, "Level of Intensity" (referred to in the guide as "Level"), measures the ride's physical intensity: that is, the amount of flipping, slamming and bouncing; and the severity of the force of gravity that the passenger is subjected to. A Level 1 ride is the most gentle; Level 5 is the most severe. Use this rating to determine whether children, seniors or coaster novices should attempt to climb aboard. The second rating is a "Star" rating, from one to five, referring to ride quality. One star is the poorest; five stars is the best. A ride rated "Level 5 ★★," indicates a very physical experience, yet extremely lacking in quality. A "Level 5 ★★★★★Super Screamer" is the wildest, most rambunctious ride, superior in design, operation, and maintenance.

These ratings are based on my own experiences riding the rides, as well as input from other coaster enthusiasts and casual fans. Unless otherwise noted, all parks listed operate seasonally, usually from spring to fall. Parks that are open early or late in the season tend to operate only on weekends and holidays during those periods. It is highly recommended that you call ahead for exact days and hours of operation, as they are subject to change at any given time.

Additionally, parks will be more than happy to provide guests with precise directions and information about accommodations in the area.

It is also recommended that you call the park to ensure that the roller coasters you desire to ride will be operational on the day of your visit. Regularly scheduled maintenance work, especially at parks that are open year-round, or a persistent mechanical problem, may leave unknowing visitors extremely disappointed. Of course, unforeseen mechanical difficulties may require that a ride be shut down on the day of your visit; if that happens, the only solution is to grin and bear it. Rides that are unavailable are usually posted each day outside the park at the ticket booths. You may also check with Guest Services.

When traveling abroad, you might want to consult a knowledgeable travel agent for more insight into theme parks and their roller coasters in the area.

AFRICA

SOUTH AFRICA

Gold Reef City, Johannesburg
1. ANACONDA, Steel Inverted; Level 4   ★★★★
2. GOLDEN LOOP, Steel Looping Shuttle; Level 5   ★★★★
3. SHAFT OF TERROR, Steel Non-looping; Level 4   ★★★★

Rantanga Junction, Chempet
1. BAR ONE BUSHWHACKER, Steel Junior; Level 3   ★★★
2. COBRA, Steel Inverted; Level 5   ★★★★
3. DIAMOND DEVIL RUN, Steel Mine Train; Level 2   ★★★

ASIA

CHINA

Ocean Park, Hong Kong (852) 25520291
1. DRAGON, Steel Looping; Level 3   ★★★
2. MINE TRAIN, Steel Mine Train; Level 2   ★★★

INDIA

Esselworld, New Delhi 91-22-869-9957
1. LITTLE DIPPER, Wood Out and Back; Level 2   ★★★

JAPAN

Central Park, Himeji-shi 0792-64-1611
1. DIAVLO, Steel Inverted; Level 5   ★★★★

Expoland, Osaka 06-877-0560
1. DAIDARASAURUS, Steel Non-Looping; Level 3   ★★★★
2. FUJIN-RAIJIN II, Steel Looping Stand-up; Level 4   ★★★
3. OROCHI, Steel Inverted; Level 5   ★★★★★
4. SPACE SALAMANDER, Steel Looping; Level 3   ★★★
5. WILD MOUSE, Steel Wild Mouse; Level 3   ★★★★

Family Land, Gotemba 05-5083-1616
1. GAMBIT, Steel Inverted; Level 5   ★★★★★
2. STAND-UP COASTER, Steel Looping Stand-up; Level 4   ★★★

Fujikyu Highlands, Osaka 0555-24-6888
1. DODONPA, Steel Non-looping; Level 4   ★★★★
    (At 106 mph, it's the world's fastest roller coaster.)
2. FUJIYAMA, Steel Non-looping; Level 5   ★★★★★ Super Screamer
3. WILD MOUSE, Compact Steel; Level 3   ★★★★

Hakkeijima Sea Paradise, Yokohama 045-788-8888
1. SURF COASTER, Steel Non-looping; Level 4   ★★★★
    (Part of this fascinating ride, extending into the Sea of Japan, is built
    on pontoons.)

Hirakata Amusement Park, Hirakata 0720-44-3475
1. ELF, Wooden Out and Back; Level 3   ★★★★

Kijima Resort, Kijima
1. JUPITER, Wood Twister; Level 4   ★★★★
    (Opened in 1993, after a lifting of restrictions regarding wooden
    structures of any significant height, this was the first wooden roller
    coaster ever to be built in Japan.)

Koraku-en Amusement Park, Tokyo 03-58-00-9999
1. GEOPANIC, Steel Enclosed; Level 3   ★★★
2. LINEAR GALE, Steel Shuttle LIM Inverted; Level 5   ★★★★★
3. ROLLER COASTER, Steel Non-looping; Level 3   ★★★

Mitsui Greenland, Arao-shi, 81-968-0012
1. ATOMIC, Steel Looping Shuttle; Level 5   ★★★
2. FUFIN-RAIJIN, Steel Looping Dual-track Stand-up; Level 5   ★★★★
3. GAO, Steel Non-looping; Level 4   ★★★★
4. GRAMPUS JET, Steel Suspended; Level 3   ★★★
5. MEGATON, Steel Looping; Level 5   ★★★
6. NIO, Steel Inverted; Level 5   ★★★★
7. SPIN MOUSE, Steel Wild Mouse; Level 3   ★★★★

Mukogaoka Amusement Park, Mukogaoka 81-449-11428
1. DIOS, Steel Non-looping; Level 4   ★★★★

Nagashima Spaland, Mei-ken 059-4-45-1111
1. CORKSCREW, Steel Looping; Level 2   ★★
2. JET COASTER, Steel Mine Train; Level 3   ★★★
3. LOOPING STAR, Steel Looping; Level 3   ★★★
4. SHUTTLE LOOP, Steel Looping Shuttle; Level 4   ★★
5. STEEL DRAGON 2000, Steel Non-looping; Level 5   ★★★★★ Super Screamer
6. ULTRA TWISTER, Steel Looping; Level 4   ★★★
7. WHITE CYCLONE, Wood Twister; Level 5   ★★★★★ Super Screamer
8. WILD MOUSE, Steel Wild Mouse; Level 3   ★★★★

Nara Dreamland, Nara 0742-23-1111
1. ASKA, Wood Out and Back; Level 3   ★★★★

Nasu Highlands, Nasu
1. BATFLYER, Steel Suspended; Level 2   ★★★
2. CAMEL COASTER, Steel Non-looping; Level 2   ★★
3. F2, Steel Inverted; Level 5   ★★★★
4. LIGHTNING, Steel Compact Portable; Level 3   ★★★★
5. SPEED BOBSLEIGH, Steel Compact Portable; Level 3   ★★★★
6. THUNDER, Steel Looping; Level 3   ★★★

Parque Espana, Osaka
1. GRAN MONTSERRAT, Steel Non-looping; Level 3   ★★★
2. PYRENEES, Steel Inverted; Level 5   ★★★★
3. SUPER EXPRESS IBERIA, Steel Enclosed; Level 3   ★★★

Seibu-en Amusement Park, Seibu-en 429-22-1371
1. LOOP SCREW, Steel Looping; Level 3   ★★★★

Space World, Kita-Kyushu-shi 81-9-36-72-3600
1. BLACK HOLE SCRAMBLE, Enclosed Steel; Level 3 ★★★
2. CLIPPER, Steel Junior; Level 2 ★★★
3. TITAN, Steel Non-looping; Level 5 ★★★★
4. VENUS, Steel Looping; Level 5 ★★★★

Summerland, Tokyo 0425-586511
1. HAYABUSA, Steel Suspended; Level 4 ★★★★
2. TORNADO, Steel Looping; Level 3 ★★★

Suzuka Circuit, Suzuka
1. BLACKOUT, Steel Inverted; Level 5 ★★★★
2. MAD COBRA, Steel Looping LIM; Level 5 ★★★★

Tobu Zoo Park, Minami Saitama Gun 81-480-93-1200
1. REGINA, Wood Out and Back; Level 4 ★★★★

Tokyo Disneyland, Urayasu 045-683-3333
1. BIG THUNDER MOUNTAIN RAILROAD, Steel Mine Train; Level 3 ★★★
2. GADGET'S GO COASTER, Compact Steel; Level 2 ★★★
3. SPACE MOUNTAIN, Steel Indoor; Level 3 ★★★

Yomiuriland, Tokyo 81-44966-1111
1. BANDIT, Steel Non-looping; Level 5 ★★★★★ Super Screamer
2. STAND-UP, Steel Stand-up; Level 4 ★★★
3. WHITE CANYON, Wood Twister; Level 3 ★★★★

KOREA

Everland, Seoul 82-31-320-5000
1. FORTRESS OF EAGLE, Steel Suspended; Level 4 ★★★★

AUSTRALIA

Australia's Wonderland, Sydney 02-9830-9100
The two wooden coasters in this park are patterned after the junior woodies and the rides known as Grizzly at the North American Paramount parks.
1. BEASTIE, Wood Junior; Level 2 ★★★
2. BUSH BEAST, Wood Twister; Level 3 ★★★
3. VAMPIRE, Steel Looping Shuttle; Level 4 ★★★

Dreamworld, Coomera 61-7-5588-1111
1.   CYCLONE, Steel Looping; Level 4   ★★★★
2.   THUNDERBOLT, Steel Looping; Level 4   ★★★★
3.   TOWER OF TERROR, Steel Non-looping Shuttle; Level 5   ★★★

Luna Park, Melbourne 1902-240-112
1.   SCENIC RAILWAY, Wood Out and Back; Level 3   ★★★

Warner Bros. Movie World, Brisbane 61-7-5573-3999
1.   LETHAL WEAPON–THE RIDE, Steel Inverted; Level 5   ★★★★

World Expo Park, Brisbane
1.   CENTRIFUGE, Steel Suspended; Level 3   ★★★
2.   SUPERNOVA, Steel Enclosed; Level 3   ★★★
3.   TITAN, Steel Looping Shuttle; Level 4   ★★★

EUROPE

AUSTRIA

Prater Park, Vienna 43-728-05-16
1.   BOOMERANG, Steel Looping Shuttle; Level 4   ★★★★
2.   DIZZY MOUSE, Steel Wild Mouse; Level 3   ★★★★
3.   HOCHSCHAUBAHN, Wood Out and Back; Level 2   ★★★
4.   MEGABLITZ, Steel Non-Looping; Level 3   ★★★
5.   SUPER-8 BAHN, Compact Steel; Level 3   ★★★
6.   WILDE MAUS, Steel Wild Mouse; Level 3   ★★★★

BELGIUM

Bobbejaanland, Kasterlee 3214-557-811
1.   AIR RACE, Steel Suspended; Level 2   ★★★
2.   LOOPING STAR, Steel Looping; Level 3   ★★★
3.   REVOLUTION, Enclosed Steel Non-looping; Level 2   ★★
4.   SPEEDY BOB, Steel Wild Mouse; Level 3   ★★★★

Six Flags Belgium, Wavre 32 10 42 16-03
1.   CALAMITY MINE, Steel Mine Train; Level 2   ★★★
2.   COBRA, Steel Looping Shuttle; Level 4   ★★★★
3.   COCCINELLE, Steel Kiddie; Level 1   ★★
4.   WEREWOLF, Wood Twister; Level 3   ★★★★

5. TORNADO, Steel Looping; Level 3   ★★
6. TURBINE, Steel Looping Shuttle; Level 4   ★★★★
7. VAMPIRE, Steel Inverted; Level 5   ★★★★

DENMARK

Bakken, Klampenborg 3963-3544
1. MINE TRAIN ULVEN, Steel Mine Train; Level 2   ★★
2. RACING, Steel Non-looping; Level 2   ★★★
3. RUTSCHEBANEN, Wood Twister; Level 3   ★★★★

Tivoli Gardens, Copenhagen 45-33-15-1001
1. KARAVANEN, Steel Junior; Level 1   ★★★
2. RUTSCHEBANEN, Wood Twister; Level 3   ★★★★
3. SLANGEN, Steel Junior; Level 1   ★★★

FINLAND

Linnanmaki Park, Helsinki 358-0-77-3991
1. SPACE EXPRESS, Enclosed Steel Non-looping; Level 3   ★★★
2. VUORISTORATA, Wood Twister; Level 4   ★★★★

Sarkanniemi Amusement Park, Tampere 358-2-2488212
1. CORKSCREW, Steel Looping; Level 3   ★★★
2. JET STAR, Compact Steel; Level 3   ★★★★
3. SPEEDY SNAKE, Steel Junior; Level 2   ★★★
4. TORNADO, Steel Inverted; Level 4   ★★★★

FRANCE

Disneyland Paris, Marne le Vallee 33-164-743000
1. BIG THUNDER MOUNTAIN RAILROAD, Steel Mine Train; Level 3   ★★★★
2. CASEY JR., Steel Junior; Level 2   ★★★
3. LE TEMPLE DE PÉRIL, Steel Looping; Level 3   ★★★
4. SPACE MOUNTAIN, Enclosed Steel Looping; Level 4   ★★★★

Parc Astérix, Plailly 33-44-623131
1. GOUDURIX, Steel Looping; Level 4   ★★★★
2. LE TRAN'S ARVERNE, Steel Junior; Level 2   ★★★
3. SERPENTIN, Steel Junior; Level 2   ★★
4. TONNERRE DE ZEUS, Wood Twister; Level 4   ★★★★★
5. TRACE DU HOURRA, Steel Bobsled; Level 3   ★★★★
6. VOL D'ICARE, Steel Junior; Level 2   ★★★

Walibi Stroumpf, Metz 33-87-519052
1. ANACONDA, Wood Out and Back; Level 4   ★★★★
2. SPACE COMET, Steel Looping; Level 3   ★★★

Walt Disney Studios Paris, Marne le Vallee 33-164-743000
1. ROCK AND ROLLER COASTER, Enclosed Steel Looping; Level 3   ★★★★

GERMANY

Europa Park, Rust 49-7822-770
1. EURO MIR, Steel Non-looping; Level 3   ★★★★
2. EUROSAT, Enclosed Steel Non-looping; Level 3   ★★★
3. MATTERHORN BLITZ, Steel Wild Mouse; Level 3   ★★★★
4. SCHWEIZER BOBBAHN, Steel Boblsed; Level 3   ★★★★
5. SILVER STAR, Steel Non-looping; Level 4   ★★★★★

Heide Park, Soltau 49-5191-5022
1. BIG LOOP, Steel Looping; Level 3   ★★★
2. COLOSSOS, Wood Out and Back; Level 4   ★★★★
3. GROTTENBLITZ, Steel Mine Train; Level 3   ★★★
4. LIMIT, Steel Inverted; Level 5   ★★★★
5. SCHWEIZER BOBBAHN, Steel Bobsled; Level 3   ★★★

Holiday Park, Hassloch 0180-5003246
1. EXPEDITION GEFORCE, Steel Non-looping; Level 5   ★★★★★ Super Screamer
2. SUPER WIRBEL, Steel Looping; Level 3   ★★★

Phantasialand, Bruhl 49-2232-36242
1. COLORADO ADVENTURE, Steel Mine Train; Level 3   ★★★
2. TEMPLE OF THE NIGHT HAWK, Enclosed Steel Non-looping; Level 2 ★★★★
3. WINJAS, Steel Wild Mouse; Level 3   ★★★★

Warner Bros. Movie World, Bottrop 49-2045-8990
1. ERASER, Steel Inverted; Level 5   ★★★★
2. LETHAL WEAPON, Steel Looping; Level 4   ★★★★
3. WILD WILD WEST, Wood Twister; Level 4   ★★★★

GREAT BRITAIN

England

Alton Towers, Staffordshire 01538-702200

Height restrictions require that no ride in this beautiful park rise above the treetops. To meet this demand, the clever folks who run the park dug pits to place their roller coasters in!

1. AIR, Steel Flying Coaster; Level 4   ★★★★★
2. BEASTIE, Steel Kiddie; Level 1   ★★
3. BLACK HOLE, Enclosed Compact Steel; Level 3   ★★★
4. CORKSCREW, Steel Looping; Level 3   ★★★
5. NEMESIS, Steel Inverted; Level 4   ★★★★
6. OBLIVION, Steel Non-looping; Level 4   ★★★★
7. RUNAWAY MINE TRAIN, Steel Mine Train; Level 2   ★★★

Blackpool Pleasure Beach, Blackpool 01253-341033

1. AVALANCHE, Steel Boblsed; Level 4   ★★★★
2. BIG DIPPER, Wood Out and Back; Level 4   ★★★★
3. GRAND NATIONAL, Wood Dual-track Out and Back; Level 4 ★★★★
4. NICKY'S CIRCUS, Steel Kiddie; Level 1   ★★
5. PEPSI MAX BIG ONE, Steel Non-looping; Level 3   ★★★
6. REVOLUTION, Steel Looping Shuttle; Level 3   ★★
7. ROLLER COASTER, Wood Out and Back; Level 3   ★★★
8. SPACE INVADERS, Enclosed Compact Steel; Level 3   ★★★★
9. STEEPLECHASE, Steel Triple-track; Level 3   ★★★★
10. WILD MOUSE, Compact Wood Twister; Level 5   ★★★★
11. ZIPPER DIPPER, Wood Junior Out and Back; Level 2   ★★★

Chessington World of Adventures, Surrey 01372-727227

1. RATTLESNAKE, Steel Wild Mouse, Level 3   ★★★
2. VAMPIRE, Steel Suspended; Level 3   ★★★

Drayton Manor, Staffordshire 01827-287979

1. KLONDIKE OLD MINE, Compact Steel Looping; Level 3   ★★★
2. SHOCKWAVE, Steel Looping Stand-up; Level 4   ★★★★
3. SUPER DRAGON COASTER, Steel Kiddie; Level 1   ★★

Dreamland Fun Park, Margate, Kent 01843-227011

1. BLUE COASTER, Steel Junior; Level 2   ★★
2. LOOPING STAR, Steel Looping; Level 3   ★★★★
3. SCENIC RAILWAY, Wood Out and Back; Level 3   ★★★
4. WILD MOUSE, Steel Wild Mouse; Level 3   ★★★

Roller Coaster Fact: The Kennywood Racer, La Fería's Serpiente de Fuego, and Blackpool's Grand National only appear to be dual-tracked racing coasters. All three are actually continuous single-track coasters, which is why trains leaving the station on one side will return to the other side at ride's end.

Flamingo Land, North Yorkshire 01653-668-287
1. BULLET, Steel Looping Shuttle; Level 5 ★★★★
2. CORKSCREW, Steel Looping; Level 3 ★★★
3. GO GATER, Steel Kiddie; Level 1 ★★
4. MAGNUM FORCE, Steel Looping; Level 5 ★★★★★
5. THUNDER MOUNTAIN, Enclosed Steel; Level 2 ★★★
6. WILD MOUSE, Steel Wild Mouse; Level 3 ★★★

Frontier Land, Morcambe 01524-410024
1. AMERICAN COASTER, Steel Kiddie; Level 1 ★★
2. BUFFALO STAMPEDE, Compact Steel Non-looping; Level 2 ★★
3. RATTLER, Steel Kiddie; Level 1 ★★
4. STAMPEDE, Steel Non-looping; Level 3 ★★★
5. TEXAS TORNADO, Wood Out and Back; Level 3 ★★★

Great Yarmouth Pleasure Beach, Norfolk 01493-844585
1. ROLLER COASTER, Wood Twister; Level 3 ★★★

Gulliver's World, Warrington 01925-444888
1. ANTELOPE, Wood Twister; Level 3 ★★★

Lightwater Valley, North Yorkshire 01765-635321
1. BATFLYER, Steel Suspended Junior; Level 2 ★★★
2. RAT, Enclosed Compact Steel; Level 3 ★★★★
3. TREETOP TWISTER, Steel Wild Mouse; Level 3 ★★★★
4. ULTIMATE, Steel Terrain; Level 4 ★★★★
5. VIPER, Compact Steel; Level 3 ★★★★

Southport Pleasure Beach, Southport 01704-532717
1. BIG APPLE, Steel Kiddie; Level 1 ★★
2. CYCLONE, Wood Twister; Level 3 ★★★

3.   KING SOLOMON'S MINES, Wood Wild Mouse; Level 4   ★★★★
4.   TRAUMATIZER, Steel Inverted; Level 5   ★★★★
5.   WILDCAT, Compact Steel Non-looping; Level 2   ★★

Thorpe Park, Surrey 01932-565298
1.   COLOSSUS, Steel Looping; Level 5   ★★★★
2.   FLYING FISH, Steel Kiddie; Level 1   ★★
3.   X:/NO WAY OUT, Enclosed Steel; Level 3   ★★★

Wales

Oakwood Leisure Park, Pembrokeshire 01834-891-373
1.   MEGAFOBIA, Wood Twister; Level 5   ★★★★★ Super Screamer

HUNGARY

Vidam Park, Budapest 343-3560
1.   HULLAMVASUT, Wood Twister; Level 2   ★★★
2.   KUKOMATIVRA, Steel Kiddie; Level 1   ★★
3.   LOOPING STAR, Steel Looping; Level 3   ★★★★

ITALY

Mirabilandia, Ravenna 39-0544-561111
1.   FAMILY ADVENTURE, Steel Junior; Level 2   ★★★
2.   KATUN, Steel Inverted; Level 4   ★★★★
3.   PAKAL, Steel Wild Mouse; Level 2   ★★★
4.   SIERRA TONANTE, Wood Twister; Level 4   ★★★★

THE NETHERLANDS

De Eftelling, Kaatsheuvel 0-416-788-111
1.   PEGASUS, Wood Twister; Level 2   ★★★
2.   PYTHON, Steel Looping; Level 2   ★★★

Six Flags Holland, Dronten 0321-329 999
1.   EL CONDOR, Steel Inverted; Level 5   ★★★
2.   FLYING DUTCHMAN, Steel Wild Mouse; Level 3   ★★★★
3.   GOLIATH, Steel Non-looping; level 4   ★★★★
4.   ROAD RUNNER, Steel Junior; Level 2   ★★★
5.   ROBIN HOOD, Wood Twister; Level 4   ★★★★
6.   SUPERMAN–THE RIDE, Steel Looping LIM; Level 5   ★★★★
7.   VIA VOLTA, Steel Looping Shuttle; Level 4   ★★★

NORWAY

TusenFryd, Vinterbro 6497-6699
1. LOOPEN, Steel Looping; Level 3   ★★★★
2. THUNDERCOASTER, Wood Out and Back; Level 3   ★★★★

SPAIN

Terra Mitica, Benidorm 00 34 96 500 43 21
1. ALUCINAKIS, Steel Junior; Level 1   ★★
2. MAGNUS COLOSSUS, Wood Out and Back; Level 4   ★★★★

Universal's Port Aventura, Tarragona 34-7779033
1. DRAGON KAHN, Steel Looping; Level 5   ★★★★★ Super Screamer
2. EL DIABLO, Steel Mine Train; Level 2   ★★
3. STAMPIDA, Wood Dual-track Twister; Level 4   ★★★★★
4. TOMAHAWK, Wood Junior Out and Back; Level 2   ★★★

Warner Bros. Movie World, San Martin de la Vega
1. BATMAN–THE RIDE, Steel Inverted; Level 5   ★★★★★ Super Screamer
2. SUPERMAN, Steel Floorless; Level 5   ★★★★★
3. TOM AND JERRY, Steel Junior; Level 2   ★★★
4. TWISTER, Steel Inverted Shuttle; Level 4   ★★★
5. WILD WILD WEST, Wood Out and Back; Level 4   ★★★★

SWEDEN

Grona Lund Park, Stockholm 46-0-8-587 501 00
1. JETLINE, Steel Non-looping; Level 4   ★★★★

Liseberg, Gothenburg 460-31-400-100
1. BALDER, Wood Twister; Level 3   ★★★
2. HANGOVER, Steel Inverted Shuttle; Level 4   ★★★★
3. LISEBERGBANEN, Steel Non-looping Terrain; Level 4   ★★★★

NORTH AMERICA

CANADA

Alberta

Calaway Park, Calgary, Alberta (403) 240-3822
1. TURN OF THE CENTURY, Steel Looping; Level 3   ★★★

Galaxyland, Edmonton, Alberta (403) 444-5300
1. AUTO SLED, Steel Non-looping; Level 2   ★★★
2. DRAGON WAGON, Steel Kiddie; Level 1   ★★
3. MINDBENDER, Steel Looping; Level 5   ★★★★

British Columbia

Playland Amusement Park, Vancouver, British Columbia (604) 255-5161
This seasonal amusement park operates as the midway for the Pacific
National Exhibition for several weeks in late summer.
1. CORKSCREW, Steel Looping; Level 3   ★★★
2. ROLLER COASTER, Wood Twister; Level 4   ★★★★
3. WILD MOUSE, Steel Wild Mouse; Level 3   ★★★

New Brunswick

Crystal Palace, Dieppe, New Brunswick (506) 859-4386
1. CRYSTAL BULLET, Steel Junior; Level 2   ★★★

Nova Scotia

Upper Clements Family Theme Park, Clementsport, Nova Scotia (902)
532-7557
1. TREE TOPPER, Wood Out and Back; Level 3   ★★★

Ontario

Chippewa Park, Thunder Bay, Ontario (807) 622-9777
1. ROLLER COASTER, Steel Junior; Level 2   ★★

Marineland, Niagara Falls, Ontario (416) 356-8250
1. DRAGON MOUNTAIN, Steel Looping; Level 3   ★★★★
2. TIVOLI, Steel Kiddie; Level 1   ★★★

Paramount Canada's Wonderland, Vaughan, Ontario (416) 832-7000
1. BAT, Steel Looping Shuttle; Level 4 ★★★
2. DRAGON FYRE, Steel Looping; Level 3 ★★★
3. FLY, Steel Wild Mouse; Level 3 ★★★
4. MIGHTY CANADIAN MINEBUSTER, Wood Out and Back; Level 4 ★★★★
5. SCOOBY'S GHOSTER COASTER, Wood Junior; Level 2 ★★★
6. SILVER STREEK, Steel Suspended Junior; Level 2 ★★★
7. SKYRIDER, Steel Stand-up; Level 4 ★★★
8. TAXI JAM, Steel Kiddie; Level 1 ★★
9. TOP GUN, Steel Inverted; Level 5 ★★★★
10. VORTEX, Steel Suspended; Level 4 ★★★★
11. WILDE BEAST, Wood Twister; Level 4 ★★★★

Quebec

La Ronde, Montreal, Quebec (514) 872-6120
1. LE VAMPIRE, Steel Inverted; Level 5 ★★★★★ Super Screamer
2. COBRA, Steel Stand-up; Level 4 ★★★★
3. LE BOOMERANG, Steel Looping Shuttle; Level 4 ★★★
4. LE DRAGON, Enclosed Steel Junior; Level 3 ★★★
5. LE MONSTRE, Wood Dual-track Twister; Level 4 ★★★★
6. LE SUPER MENAGE, Steel Looping; Level 3 ★★★
7. LES PETITES MONTAGNES RUSSES, Steel Kiddie; Level 1 ★★★

Les Galleries Capitale, Quebec City, Quebec (418) 627-5800
1. CAPITAL EXPRESS, Steel Junior; Level 2 ★★★

MEXICO

La Feria Chapultepec Magico, Mexico City 52-5-230-2121
1. CASCABEL, Steel Looping Shuttle; Level 4 ★★★★
2. RATON LOCO, Steel Wild Mouse; Level 3 ★★★★
3. SERPIENTE DE FUEGO, Wood Dual-track Out and Back; Level 4 ★★★★
4. TORNADO, Compact Steel; Level 3 ★★★

Six Flags Mexico, Mexico City 52-5-645-3335
1. BATMAN–THE RIDE, Steel Inverted; Level 5 ★★★★
2. BOOMERANG, Steel Looping Shuttle; Level 4 ★★★
3. CATARINA VOLADORA, Steel Junior; Level 1 ★★★
4. MEDUSA, Wood Twister; Level 5 ★★★★★ Super Screamer
5. ROLLER SKATER, Steel Junior; Level 2 ★★★

UNITED STATES

Alabama

Waterville, USA, Gulf Shores, Alabama (205) 948-2106
1. CANNONBALL, Wood Out and Back; Level 3   ★★★★

Visionland, Bessemer, Alabama (205) 481-4750
1. RAMPAGE, Wood Twister; Level 5   ★★★★★ Super Screamer

Arizona

Castles and Coasters, Phoenix, Arizona (602) 997-7576
1. DESERT STORM, Steel Looping; Level 3   ★★
2. PATRIOT, Steel Junior; Level 1   ★★★

Arkansas

Magic Springs, Hot Springs, Arkansas 501-624-0100
1. ARKANSAS TWISTER, Wood Out and Back; Level 3   ★★★★
2. BIG BAD JOHN, Steel Mine Train; Level 3   ★★★★
3. DIAMOND MINE RUN, Steel Kiddie; Level 2   ★★★
4. TWIST AND SHOUT, Steel Wild Mouse; Level 2   ★★★
5. ZYKLON, Compact Steel; Level 2   ★★

California

Belmont Park, San Diego, California (619) 488-1549
Belmont Park was at one time a full-fledged seaside amusement park. It closed in the 1970s, leaving only the classic wooden roller coaster standing. Local preservation efforts rebuilt the coaster, and it now operates as a stand-alone attraction, together with a carousel, as part of a shopping center. Attractions at this park are open daily, year-round.
1. GIANT DIPPER, Wood Twister; Level 4   ★★★★

Disneyland, Anaheim, California (714) 999-4000
1. BIG THUNDER MOUNTAIN RAILROAD, Steel Mine Train; Level 2   ★★★★
2. GADGET'S GO COASTER, Steel Junior; Level 1   ★★★
3. MATTERHORN BOBLSED, Dual-track Steel Non-looping; Level 2   ★★★★
4. SPACE MOUNTAIN, Enclosed Steel Non-looping; Level 3   ★★★★

Disney's California Adventure, Anaheim, California (714) 999-4000
1. CALIFORNIA SCREAMIN', Steel Looping LIM; Level 4   ★★★★
2. MULHOLLAND MADNESS; Steel Wild Mouse; Level 3   ★★★★

Knott's Berry Farm, Buena Park, California (714) 827-1776
1. BOOMERANG, Steel Looping Shuttle; Level 4   ★★★
2. GHOSTRIDER, Wood Twister; Level 4   ★★★★★   Super Screamer
3. JAGUAR, Steel Non-looping; Level 2   ★★★
4. MONTEZOOMA'S REVENGE, Steel Looping Shuttle; Level 4   ★★★★
5. TIMBERLINE TWISTER, Steel Kiddie; Level 1   ★★★
6. XCELERATOR, Steel Non-looping LIM; Level 5   ★★★★

Pacific Pier, Santa Monica, California (310) 260-8744
1. WEST COASTER, Steel Non-looping; Level 2   ★★

Paramount's Great America, Santa Clara, California (408) 988-1800
Opened in 1976 by the Marriott Hotel Corporation, the park changed hands several times before being purchased by Paramount, primarily known for its motion picture productions.
1. DEMON, Steel Looping; Level 3   ★★★
2. GREASED LIGHTNIN', Steel Looping Shuttle; Level 3   ★★★★
3. GREEN SLIME MINE CAR, Steel Junior; Level 1   ★★★
4. GRIZZLY, Wood Twister; Level 3   ★★★
5. INVERTIGO, Steel Inverted Shuttle; Level 4   ★★★★
6. PSYCHO MOUSE, Steel Wild Mouse; Level 3   ★★★
7. STEALTH, STEEL Flying Coaster; Level 5   ★★★★
8. TAXI JAM, Steel Kiddie; Level 2   ★★
9. TOP GUN, Steel Inverted; Level 4   ★★★★
10. VORTEX, Steel Stand-up; Level 4   ★★★★

Santa Cruz Beach Boardwalk, Santa Cruz, California (408) 423-5590
1. GIANT DIPPER, Wood Twister; Level 4   ★★★★
2. HURRICANE, Steel Non-looping; Level 3   ★★★★

Scandia Family Fun Center, Ontario, California (909) 390-3092
1. SCANDIA SCREAMER, Steel Non-looping: Level 3   ★★★

Six Flags Magic Mountain, Valencia, California (818) 992-0884
Open weekends year-round, daily spring through fall.
1. BATMAN–THE RIDE, Steel Inverted; Level 5 ★★★★★ Super Screamer
2. CANYON BLASTER, Steel Kiddie; Level 1   ★★★
3. COLOSSUS, Wood Dual-track Out and Back; Level 4   ★★★★
4. DÉJÀ VU, Steel Inverted Shuttle; Level 4   ★★★★
5. FLASHBACK, Steel Non-looping; Level 5   ★★
6. GOLD RUSHER, Mine Train; Level 2   ★★★
7. GOLIATH, Steel Non-looping; Level 5   ★★★★

Santa Cruz's Giant Dipper is a National Historic Landmark. (Courtesy of Dennis McNulty)

8. GOLIATH JR., Steel Kiddie; Level 1   ★★
9. NINJA, Steel Suspended; Level 4   ★★★★
10. PSYCLONE, Wood Twister; Level 4   ★★★★
11. REVOLUTION, Steel Looping; Level 4   ★★★★
12. RIDDLER'S REVENGE, Steel Stand-up; Level 4   ★★★★
13. SUPERMAN–THE ESCAPE, Steel Non-looping Shuttle; Level 4   ★★★★
14. VIPER, Steel Looping; Level 5   ★★★★
15. X, Steel Looping; Level 5   ★★★★

Six Flags Marine World, Vallejo, California (707) 644-4000
1. BOOMERANG, Steel Looping Shuttle; Level 4   ★★★
2. COBRA, Steel Junior; Level 2   ★★★
3. KONG, Steel Inverted; Level 5   ★★★
4. MEDUSA, Steel Floorless; Level 5   ★★★★★ Super Screamer
5. ROADRUNNER EXPRESS, Steel Kiddie; Level 1   ★★
6. ROAR, Wood Twister; Level 5   ★★★★★ Super Screamer
7. V2 VERTICAL VELOCITY, Steel Shuttle; Level 5   ★★★★

The Lakeside Cyclone, Denver, circling over its art-deco style station. (Courtesy of Bobby Nagy)

Colorado

Lakeside Amusement Park, Denver, Colorado (303) 477-1621
1. CYCLONE, Wood Twister; Level 3   ★★★★
2. WILD CHIPMUNK, Compact Steel Non-looping; Level 4   ★★★★

Six Flags Elitch Gardens, Denver, Colorado (303) 595-4386
1. BOOMERANG, Steel Looping Shuttle; Level 4   ★★★
2. FLYING COASTER, Steel Suspended; Level 3   ★★★
3. GREAT CHASE, Steel Kiddie; Level 1   ★★
4. MIND ERASER, Steel Inverted; Level 5   ★★★★
5. SIDEWINDER, Steel Looping Shuttle; Level 3   ★★
6. TWISTER II, Wood Twister; Level 4   ★★★★

Connecticut

Lake Compounce, Bristol, Connecticut (860) 583-3631
The oldest continuously operating amusement park in the country, it got a major face lift for the 1997 season, ensuring that it will be around for many generations to come.
1. BOULDER DASH, Wood Out and Back; Level 3   ★★★★
2. WILDCAT, Wood Twister; Level 4   ★★★
3. ZOOMERANG, Steel Looping Shuttle; Level 4   ★★★

Kumba roars through
Busch Gardens,
Tampa. (Courtesy of
Bobby Nagy)

Florida

Busch Gardens, Tampa, Florida (813) 987-5000
The combination of Kumba and Montu provides this park with an un-
beatable pair—these are two of the best steel roller coasters currently operating. Open daily, year-round.
1. KUMBA, Steel Looping; Level 5   ★★★★★ Super Screamer
2. GWAZI, Wood Dual-track Twister; Level 4   ★★★★
3. MONTU, Steel Inverted; Level 5   ★★★★★ Super Screamer
4. PYTHON, Steel Looping; Level 3   ★★
5. SCORPION, Steel Looping; Level 3   ★★★

Disney MGM Studios at Walt Disney World, Lake Buena Vista, Florida
(407) 828-2100
1. ROCK AND ROLLER COASTER, Steel Enclosed Looping; Level 3   ★★★★

Disney's Animal Kingdom at Walt Disney World, Lake Buena Vista, Florida
  (407) 828-2100
1. PRIMEVAL WHIRL, Steel Wild Mouse; Level 3   ★★★★

The Magic Kingdom at Walt Disney World, Lake Buena Vista, Florida
  (407) 828-2100
Open daily, year-round.
1. THE BARNSTORMER, Steel Junior; Level 1   ★★★
2. BIG THUNDER MOUNTAIN RAILROAD, Mine Train; Level 2   ★★★★
3. SPACE MOUNTAIN, Enclosed Steel Non-looping; Level 2   ★★★

Miracle Strip Amusement Park, Panama City, Florida (904) 234-3333
1. STARLINER, Wood Out and Back; Level 3   ★★★★

Old Town, Kissimmee, Florida (407) 396-4888
1. WINDSTORM, Compact Steel; Level 3   ★★★★

Seaworld, Orlando, Florida (407) 363-2200
1. KRAKEN, Steel Floorless; Level 4   ★★★★★

Universal Studios Islands of Adventure, Orlando, Florida (407) 363-8000
1. DUELING DRAGONS, Steel Dual-tracked Inverted; Level 4   ★★★★
2. FLYING UNICORN, Steel Junior; Level 2   ★★★
3. INCREDIBLE HULK, Steel Looping; Level 5   ★★★★★
4. PTERANODON FLYERS, Steel Suspended Junior; Level 2   ★★★

Georgia

Lake Winnepesaukah, Rossville, Georgia (770) 866-5681
1. CANNON BALL, Wood Out and Back; Level 3   ★★★★
2. WACKY WORM, Steel Kiddie; Level 1   ★★

Six Flags Over Georgia, Atlanta, Georgia (770) 948-9290
1. BATMAN–THE RIDE, Steel Inverted; Level 5   ★★★★★ Super Screamer
2. DAHLONEGA MINE TRAIN, Steel Mine Train; Level 2   ★★★
3. DÉJÀ VU, Steel Inverted Shuttle; Level 4   ★★★★
4. GEORGIA CYCLONE, Wood Twister; Level 5   ★★★★★ Super Screamer
5. GEORGIA SCORCHER, Steel Stand-up; Level 4   ★★★★
6. GREAT AMERICAN SCREAM MACHINE, Wood Out and Back;
    Level 4   ★★★★
7. MIND BENDER, Steel Looping; Level 5   ★★★★★ Super Screamer
8. NINJA, Steel Looping; Level 5   ★★★
9. SUPERMAN ULTIMATE FLIGHT, Steel Flying Coaster; Level 5   ★★★★

Wild Adventures, Valdosta, Georgia (800) 808-0872
1. ANT FARM EXPRESS, Steel Junior; Level 2   ★★★
2. BOOMERANG, Steel Looping Shuttle; Level 4   ★★★
3. BUG OUT, Steel Wild Mouse; Level 3   ★★★
4. CHEETAH, Wood Out and Back; Level 4   ★★★★
5. GOLD RUSH, Steel Junior; Level 2   ★★★
6. HANGMAN, Steel Inverted; Level 5   ★★★★
7. TIGER TERROR, Steel Kiddie; Level 1   ★★

Idaho

Silverwood Theme Park, Athol, Idaho (208) 772-0515
1. GRAVITY DEFYING CORKSCREW, Steel Looping; Level 2   ★★
2. TIMBER TERROR, Wood Out and Back; Level 3   ★★★★
3. TREMORS, Wood Out and Back; Level 4   ★★★★

Illinois

Hillcrest Park, Lake Zurich, Illinois (708) 438-0140
Park open only for private picnics.
1. LITTLE DIPPER, Wood Junior; Level 1   ★★★

Kiddieland, Melrose Park, Illinois (708) 343-8003
1. LITTLE DIPPER, Wood Junior; Level 1   ★★★

Six Flags Great America, Gurnee, Illinois (708) 249-1776
1. AMERICAN EAGLE, Wood Dual-track Out and Back; Level 4   ★★★★
2. BATMAN–THE RIDE, Steel Inverted; Level 5   ★★★★★ Super Screamer
3. DÉJÀ VU, Steel Inverted Shuttle; Level 4   ★★★★
4. DEMON, Steel Looping; Level 3   ★★★
5. IRON WOLF, Steel Stand-up; Level 5   ★★★★
6. RAGING BULL, Steel Non-looping; Level 5   ★★★★★
7. SHOCK WAVE, Steel Looping; Level 5   ★★★★
8. SPACELY'S SPROCKET ROCKETS, Steel Kiddie; Level 2   ★★★
9. V2 VERTICAL VELOCITY, Steel Shuttle; Level 5   ★★★★
10. VIPER, Wood Twister; Level 4   ★★★★
11. WHIZZER, Steel Non-looping; Level 2   ★★★★

Indiana

Holiday World, Santa Claus, Indiana (812) 937-4401
1. HOWLER, Steel Kiddie; Level 1   ★★★
2. LEGEND, Wood Terrain; Level 4   ★★★★★ Super Screamer
3. RAVEN, Wood Terrain; Level 4   ★★★★★ Super Screamer

Indiana Beach, Monticello, Indiana (219) 583-4141
1. CORNBALL EXPRESS, Wood Out and Back; Level 3   ★★★★
2. GALAXIE, Compact Steel; Level 2   ★★
3. HOOSIER HURRICANE, Wood Out and Back; Level 4   ★★★★
4. SUPERSTITION MOUNTAIN, Wood Gravity Dark Ride; Level 2   ★★★
5. TIG'RR, Compact Steel; Level 3   ★★★

Iowa

Adventureland, Des Moines, Iowa (515) 266-2121
1. DRAGON, Steel Looping; Level 4   ★★
2. OUTLAW, Wood Twister; Level 3   ★★★★
3. TORNADO, Wood Out and Back; Level 3   ★★★★
4. UNDERGROUND, Wood Gravity Dark Ride; Level 1   ★★★★

Arnolds Park, Arnolds Park, Iowa (712) 332-7781
1. GIANT COASTER, Wood Out and Back; Level 3   ★★★
2. LITTLE COASTER, Steel Kiddie; Level 1   ★

Kansas

Joyland Amusement Park, Wichita, Kansas (316) 684-0179
1. ROLLER COASTER, Wood Out and Back; Level 3   ★★★

Kentucky

Six Flags Kentucky Kingdom, Louisville, Kentucky (502) 366-2231
1. CHANG, Steel Stand-up; Level 5   ★★★★★
2. ROAD RUNNER EXPRESS, Steel Wild Mouse; Level 3   ★★★
3. ROLLER SKATER, Steel Junior; Level 1   ★★★
4. T^2 (TERROR TO THE SECOND POWER), Steel Inverted; Level 5   ★★★★
5. THUNDER RUN, Wood Twister; Level 4   ★★★★
6. TWISTED SISTERS, Wood Dual-track Twister; Level 4   ★★★★

Louisiana

Jazzland, New Orleans, Louisiana
1. MEGA ZEPH, Wood Out and Back; Level 3   ★★★★
2. MUSKRAT SCRAMBLE, Steel Wild Mouse; Level 3   ★★★
3. REX'S RAILRUNNER, Steel Junior; Level 2   ★★★
4. ZYDECO SCREAM, Steel Looping Shuttle; Level 4   ★★★

Maine

Funtown USA, Saco, Maine (800) 878-2900
1. Excalibur, Wood Out and Back; Level 3　★★★

Maryland

Six Flags America, Largo, Maryland (301) 249-1500
1. BATWING, Steel Flying Coaster; Level 5　★★★★
2. GREAT CHASE, Steel Kiddie; Level 1　★★★
3. JOKER'S JINX, Steel Looping LIM; Level 5　★★★★
4. MIND ERASER, Steel Inverted; Level 5　★★★★
5. ROAR, Wood Twister; Level 4　★★★★
6. SUPERMAN RIDE OF STEEL, Steel Non-looping; Level 5　★★★★★
   Super Screamer
7. TWO FACE, Steel Inverted Shuttle; Level 4　★★★★
8. WILD ONE, Wood Out and Back; Level 3　★★★★

Massachusetts

Six Flags New England, Agawam, Massachusetts (413) 786-9300
1. CYCLONE, Wood Twister; Level 5　★★★★★ Super Screamer
2. FLASHBACK, Steel Looping Shuttle; Level 4　★★★
3. GREAT CHASE, Steel Kiddie; Level 1　★★★
4. MIND ERASER, Steel Inverted; Level 5　★★★★
5. POISON IVY'S TWISTED TRAIN, Steel Junior; Level 2　★★★
6. SUPERMAN RIDE OF STEEL, Steel Non-looping; Level 5　★★★★★
   Super Screamer
7. THUNDERBOLT, Wood Twister; Level 3　★★★★
8. BATMAN—THE DARK NIGHT, Steel Floorless; Level 4　★★★★

Michigan

Michigan's Adventure, Muskegon, Michigan (616) 766-3377
1. CORKSCREW, Steel Looping; Level 3　★★
2. SHIVERING TIMBERS, Wood Out and Back; Level 5　★★★★★ Super
   Screamer
3. WOLVERINE WILDCAT, Wood Twister; Level 3　★★★★
4. ZACH'S ZOOMER, Wood Junior; Level 2　★★★

Minnesota

Knott's Camp Snoopy, Bloomington, Minnesota (612) 883-8600
1. RIPSAW, Steel Non-looping; Level 1　★★★

Valleyfair!, Shakopee, Minnesota (612) 445-7600
1. CORKSCREW, Steel Looping; Level 3 ★★★
2. EXCALIBUR, Steel Non-looping; Level 3 ★★★
3. HIGH ROLLER, Wood Out and Back; Level 3 ★★★
4. MAD MOUSE, Steel Wild Mouse; Level 3 ★★★
5. MILD THING, Steel Kiddie; Level 2 ★★
6. WILD THING, Steel Non-looping; Level 4 ★★★★

Missouri

Silver Dollar City, Branson, Missouri (417) 338-2611
1. FIRE IN THE HOLE, Steel Gravity Dark Ride; Level 3 ★★★★
2. RUNAWAY ORE CART, Steel Kiddie; Level 1 ★★★
3. THUNDERATION, Steel Mine Train; Level 4 ★★★★
4. WILDFIRE, Steel Looping; Level 4 ★★★★

Six Flags St. Louis, Allenton, Missouri (314) 938-5300
1. ACME GRAVITY POWERED ROLLER RIDE, Steel Kiddie; Level 1 ★★
2. BATMAN–THE RIDE, Steel Inverted; Level 5 ★★★★★ Super Screamer
3. BOSS, WOOD TERRAIN; Level 5 ★★★★★ Super Screamer
4. MR. FREEZE, Steel Looping Shuttle LIM; Level 5 ★★★★
5. NINJA, Steel Looping; Level 4 ★★★
6. RIVER KING MINE RIDE, Steel Mine Train; Level 2 ★★★★
7. SCREAMIN' EAGLE, Wood Out and Back; Level 4 ★★★★★ Super Screamer

Worlds of Fun, Kansas City, Missouri (816) 454-4545
1. BOOMERANG, Steel Looping Shuttle; Level 4 ★★★
2. MAMBA, Steel Non-looping; Level 4 ★★★★
3. ORIENT EXPRESS, Steel Looping; Level 4 ★★★★
4. TIMBER WOLF, Wood Twister; Level 4 ★★★★
5. WACKY WORM, Steel Kiddie; Level 1 ★★★

Nevada

All parks and attractions listed are part of large casino-resort hotels

Buffalo Bill's Resort and Casino, Stateline, Nevada ((702) 382-1212
1. DESPERADO, Steel Non-looping; Level 5 ★★★★

Grand Slam Canyon, Las Vegas, Nevada (702) 794-3939
1. CANYON BLASTER, Steel Looping; Level 3 ★★★

Nascar Café, Las Vegas, Nevada (702) 734-7223
1.   SPEED, Steel Looping Shuttle LIM; Level 5   ★★★★

New York, New York Hotel and Casino, Las Vegas, Nevada (702) 740-6969
1.   MANHATTAN EXPRESS, Steel Looping; Level 5   ★★

Stratosphere Tower, Las Vegas, Nevada (702) 382-4446
1.   HIGH ROLLER, Steel Junior; Level 3   ★★★

New Hampshire

Canobie Lake Park, Salem, New Hampshire (603) 893-3506
1.   CANOBIE CORKSCREW, Steel Looping; Level 3   ★★
2.   GALAXIE, Compact Steel; Level 2   ★★★
3.   YANKEE CANNONBALL, Wood Out and Back; Level 3   ★★★★

Superman Ride of Steel.
(Courtesy of Six Flags New England)

New Jersey

Casino Pier, Seaside Heights, New Jersey (732) 793-6488
1. STAR JET, Compact Steel; Level 4   ★★★★
2. WILD MOUSE, Steel Wild Mouse; Level 3   ★★★★
3. WIZARD'S CAVERN, Compact Enclosed Steel; Level 3   ★★★

Clementon Lake Park, Clementon, New Jersey (856) 783-0263
1. JACK RABBIT, Wood Twister; Level 3   ★★★

Morey's Piers, The Wildwoods, New Jersey (609) 729-3700
1. DO WOPPER, Steel Wild Mouse; Level 2   ★★★
2. FLITZER, Steel Junior; Level 1   ★★
3. GOLDEN NUGGET MINE RIDE, Steel Gravity Dark Ride; Level 2   ★★★★
4. GREAT NOR'EASTER, Steel Inverted; Level 5   ★★★★
5. GREAT WHITE, Wood Twister; Level 4   ★★★★
6. RC-48, Steel Compact; Level 3   ★★★★
7. ROLLIES COASTER, Steel Compact; Level 2   ★★★
8. SEA SERPENT, Steel Looping Shuttle; Level 4   ★★★

Playland, Ocean City, New Jersey (609) 399-4751
1. FLITZER, Compact Steel; Level 1   ★★
2. KIDDIE COASTER, Steel Kiddie; Level 1   ★★
3. PYTHON, Steel Looping; Level 3   ★★★
4. WILD MOUSE, Steel Wild Mouse; Level 2   ★★★★

The Great White, The Wildwoods, N.J., is the first seaside wooden coaster built in almost forty years. (Courtesy of Bobby Nagy)

Batman and Robin–The Chiller. (Courtesy of Six Flags Great Adventure)

Six Flags Great Adventure, Jackson, New Jersey (732) 928-2000
1. BATMAN AND ROBIN–THE CHILLER, Steel Dual-track LIM Shuttle; Level 5   ★★★★★ Super Screamer
2. BATMAN–THE RIDE, Steel Inverted; Level 5   ★★★★★ Super Screamer
3. BLACKBEARD'S LOST TREASURE TRAIN, Steel Junior; Level 2   ★★★★
4. GREAT AMERICAN SCREAM MACHINE, Steel Looping; Level 5   ★★★★
5. MEDUSA, Steel Floorless; Level 5   ★★★★★ Super Screamer
6. NITRO, Steel Non-looping; Level 5   ★★★★★ Super Screamer
7. ROAD RUNNER RAILWAY, Steel Kiddie; Level 2   ★★★
8. ROLLING THUNDER, Wood Dual-track Out and Back; Level 3   ★★★
9. RUNAWAY TRAIN, Steel Mine Train; Level 3   ★★★
10. SKULL MOUNTAIN, Enclosed Steel Junior; Level 3   ★★★★
11. VIPER, Steel Looping; Level 5   ★★★

New York

Adventureland, East Farmingdale, New York (516) 694-6868
1. HURRICANE, Steel Junior; Level 2   ★★★

Coney Island's Astroland, Brooklyn, New York (718) 265-2100
1. CYCLONE, Wood Twister; Level 5   ★★★★★ Super Screamer
2. BIG APPLE, Steel Kiddie; Level 1   ★★

Roller Coaster Fact: To best display the three-projector wide-screen process known as Cinerama in the film *This Is Cinerama*, a roller coaster was used. The coaster, Atom Smasher (located at the defunct Rockaway's Playland in Queens, New York), was a last-minute stand in. The filmmakers originally intended to use the nearby Coney Island Cyclone, but they found that ride too wild to mount the three cameras needed for the Cinerama process.

The Great Escape, Lake George, New York (518) 792-6568
1. ALPINE BOBSLED, Steel Bobsled; Level 2   ★★★
2. BOOMERANG, Steel Looping Shuttle; Level 4   ★★★
3. COMET, Wood Out and Back; Level 5   ★★★★★ Super Screamer
4. NIGHTMARE AT CRACKAXEL CANYON, Enclosed Steel Compact; Level 2 ★★★
5. STEAMIN' DEMON, Steel Looping; Level 4   ★★

Playland, Rye, New York (914) 813-7000
The first totally planned amusement park, now a National Historic Landmark.
1. DRAGON COASTER, Wood Twister; Level 3   ★★★
2. FAMILY FLYER, Steel Junior; Level 2   ★★★
3. HURRICANE, Steel Compact; Level 3   ★★★
4. KIDDIE COASTER, Wood Kiddie; Level 1   ★★★

Sea Breeze, Rochester, New York (716) 323-1900
1. BEAR TRAX, Steel Kiddie; Level 1   ★★★
2. BOBSLEDS, Steel Junior; Level 2   ★★★
3. JACK RABBIT, Wood Out and Back; Level 3   ★★★★
4. QUANTUM LOOP, Steel Looping; Level 3   ★★★

Six Flags Darien Lake, Corfu, New York (716) 599-4641
1. BOOMERANG COAST TO COASTER, Steel Looping Shuttle; Level 4   ★★★
2. BRAIN TEASER, Steel Kiddie; Level 2   ★★
3. MIND ERASER, Steel Inverted; Level 5   ★★★★
4. PREDATOR, Wood Twister; Level 4   ★★★★
5. SUPERMAN RIDE OF STEEL, Steel Non-looping; Level 5   ★★★★★ Super Screamer
6. VIPER, Steel Looping; Level 4   ★★★

Comet at Lake George's Great Escape. (Courtesy of Doug Brehm)

North Carolina

Ghost Town in the Sky, Maggie Valley, North Carolina (704) 926-1140
1. RED DEVIL, Steel Looping; Level 2   ★★

Paramount's Carowinds, Charlotte, North Carolina (704) 588-2606
1. CAROLINA CYCLONE, Steel Looping; Level 3   ★★★
2. CAROLINA GOLD RUSHER, Mine Train; Level 2   ★★★
3. FLYING SUPER SATURATOR, Steel Junior Suspended; Level 2   ★★★★
4. HURLER, Wood Twister; Level 4   ★★★★
5. RICOCHET, Steel Wild Mouse; Level 3   ★★★★
6. SCOOBY DOO'S GHOSTER COASTER, Wood Junior; Level 2   ★★★
7. TAXI JAM, Steel Kiddie; Level 1   ★★★
8. THUNDER ROAD, Wood Dual-track Out and Back; Level 4   ★★★★
9. TOP GUN, Steel Inverted; Level 4   ★★★★★
10. VORTEX, Steel Stand-up; Level 4   ★★★★

Ohio

Americana Amusement Park, Middletown, Ohio (513) 539-7339
1. SCREECHIN' EAGLE, Wood Out and Back; Level 4   ★★★
2. SERPENT, Compact Steel; Level 2   ★★★

Cedar Point, Sandusky, Ohio (419) 626-0830
Located on a Lake Erie peninsula, this is the world's best self-contained
amusement park, housing more rides than any other, as well as the most

roller coasters of any place in the world. In addition to the amusement park, the peninsula also features several full-service restaurants, a marina, two hotels, a campground, a water park, and beach swimming, all part of the Cedar Point Resort Complex.

1. BLUE STREAK, Wood Out and Back; Level 3   ★★★★
2. CEDAR CREAK MINE RIDE, Steel Mine Train; Level 2   ★★★
3. CORKSCREW, Steel Looping; Level 3   ★★★
4. DISASTER TRANSPORT, Enclosed Bobsled; Level 2   ★★★
5. GEMINI, Steel Dual-track Non-looping; Level 4   ★★★★
6. IRON DRAGON, Steel Suspended; Level 2   ★★★
7. JR. GEMINI, Steel Kiddie; Level 1   ★★
8. MAGNUM XL-200, Steel Non-looping; Level 5   ★★★★★ Super Screamer
9. MANTIS, Steel Stand-up; Level 5   ★★★★★ Super Screamer
10. MEAN STREAK, Wood Twister; Level 5   ★★★★
11. MILLENNIUM FORCE, Steel Non-looping; Level 5 ★★★★★ Super Screamer
12. RAPTOR, Steel Inverted; Level 5   ★★★★★ Super Screamer
13. WICKED TWISTER, Steel Shuttle LIM; Level 5   ★★★★★
14. WILDCAT, Steel Compact; Level 2   ★★★
15. WOODSTOCK'S EXPRESS, Steel Junior; Level 2   ★★★

Paramount's Kings Island, Cincinnati, Ohio (513) 398-5600
1. ADVENTURE EXPRESS, Mine Train; Level 3   ★★★★
2. BEAST, Wood Terrain; Level 5   ★★★★★ Super Screamer
3. BEASTIE, Wood Junior; Level 2   ★★★
4. FACE/OFF, Steel Inverted Shuttle; Level 4   ★★★
5. FLIGHT OF FEAR, Enclosed Looping Steel; Level 5   ★★★★★
6. KING COBRA, Steel Stand-up; Level 4   ★★★
7. RACER, Wood Dual-track Out and Back; Level 3   ★★★★
8. RUGRATS RUNAWAY REPTAR, Steel Inverted Junior; Level 2   ★★★
9. SCOOBY'S GHOSTER COASTER, Steel Suspended; Level 2   ★★★

Roller Coaster Fact: Cincinnati, Ohio's Coney Island Wildcat served as the inspiration for four modern roller coasters: Wilde Beast at Paramount Canada's Wonderland, the Grizzly rides at Paramount's Kings Dominion and Paramount's Great America, and the Bush Beast at Australia's Wonderland.

10. Son of Beast, Wood Looping Twister; Level 5   ★★★★
11. Top Cat's Taxi Jam, Steel Kiddie; Level 1   ★★
12. Top Gun, Steel Suspended; Level 5   ★★★★★ Super Screamer
13. Vortex, Steel Looping; Level 5   ★★★★

Six Flags Worlds of Adventure, Aurora, Illinois (330) 562-7131
 1. Batman Knight Flight, Steel Floorless; Level 5   ★★★★★ Super Screamer
 2. Big Dipper, Wood Out and Back; Level 3   ★★★★
 3. Double Loop, Steel Looping; Level 3   ★★★
 4. Mind Eraser, Steel Looping Shuttle; Level 4   ★★★
 5. Raging Wolf Bobs, Wood Twister; Level 3   ★★★
 6. Roadrunner Express, Steel Junior; Level 2   ★★★
 7. Serial Thriller, Steel Inverted; Level 5   ★★★★
 8. Superman Ultimate Escape, Steel Shuttle LIM; Level 4   ★★★★
 9. Villain, Wood Twister; Level 4   ★★★★
10. X-Flight, Steel Flying Coaster; Level 5   ★★★★

Stricker's Grove, Ross, Ohio (513) 521-9747
1. Comet, Wood Junior; Level 2   ★★★
2. Teddy Bear, Steel Kiddie; Level 1   ★★
3. Tornado, Wood Twister; Level 3   ★★★

Wyandot Lake, Powell, Ohio (614) 889-9283
1. Sea Dragon, Wood Junior; Level 2   ★★★

Oklahoma

Bell's Amusement Park, Tulsa, Oklahoma (918) 744-1991
1. Zingo, Wood Out and Back; Level 3   ★★★

Frontier City, Oklahoma City, Oklahoma (405) 478-2412
1. Diamond Back, Steel Looping Shuttle; Level 3   ★★
2. Nightmare Mine, Enclosed Steel Compact; Level 2   ★★★
3. Silver Bullet, Steel Looping; Level 3   ★★★★
4. Wild Kitty, Steel Kiddie; Level 1   ★★★
5. Wildcat, Wood Out and Back; Level 4   ★

Oregon

Enchanted Forest, Turner, Oregon (503) 363-3060
1. Ice Mountain Bobsled, Steel Terrain; Level 2   ★★★

Oaks Amusement Park, Portland, Oregon (503) 233-5777
1. LOOPING STAR, Steel Looping; Level 3   ★★★
2. MONSTER MOUSE, Compact Steel Non-looping; Level 2   ★★
3. TORNADO, Compact Steel Non-looping; Level 2   ★★

Thrillville, USA, Turner, Oregon (503) 363-4095
1. RIPPER, Compact Steel; Level 3   ★★★

Pennsylvania

Conneaut Lake Park, Conneaut Lake Park, Pennsylvania (814) 382-5115
1. BLUE STREAK, Wood Out and Back; Level 4   ★★★

Dorney Park, Allentown, Pennsylvania (610) 395-3724
1. HERCULES, Wood Terrain; Level 5   ★★★
2. LASER, Steel Looping; Level 4   ★★★★
3. LITTLE LASER, Steel Kiddie; Level 1   ★★
4. STEEL FORCE, Steel Non-looping; Level 5   ★★★★★ Super Screamer
5. TALON, Steel Inverted; Level 4   ★★★★
6. THUNDER HAWK, Wood Twister; Level 4   ★★★★
7. WILD MOUSE, Steel Wild Mouse; Level 3   ★★★
8. WOODSTOCK'S EXPRESS, Steel Kiddie; Level 2   ★★★

Dutch Wonderland, Lancaster, Pennsylvania (717) 291-1888
1. JOUST, Steel Junior; Level 2   ★★★
2. SKY PRINCESS, Wood Out and Back; Level 2   ★★★

Hersheypark, Hershey, Pennsylvania (717) 534-3900
1. COMET, Wood Out and Back; Level 3   ★★★★
2. GREAT BEAR, Steel Inverted; Level 3   ★★★
3. LIGHTNING RACER, Wood Dual-track Twister; Level 4   ★★★★★
   Super Screamer

Roller Coaster Fact: The Conneaut Lake (Pennsylvania) Blue Streak begins with a dark tunnel, which park personnel call the "Skunk Tunnel" because local skunks take up residence there. Several have been known to find themselves on the track when a train passes through, offering riders an aromatically enhanced ride.

Hercules, built into a hillside at Dorney Park, is a good example of a terrain ride. (Courtesy of Dorney Park)

4. ROLLER SOAKER, Steel Suspended Junior; Level 2 ★★★
5. SIDEWINDER, Steel Looping Shuttle; Level 4 ★★★
6. SOOPERDOOPERLOOPER, Steel Looping; Level 2 ★★★
7. TRAILBLAZER, Steel Mine Train; Level 2 ★★
8. WILD MOUSE, Steel Wild Mouse; Level 3 ★★★★
9. WILDCAT, Wood Twister; Level 5 ★★★★★ Super Screamer

The Kennywood Racer.
(Courtesy of Bobby Nagy)

Idlewild Park, Ligonier, Pennsylvania (412) 238-3666
1. Rollo Coaster, Wood Terrain; Level 2 ★★★
2. Wild Mouse, Steel Wild Mouse; Level 3 ★★★

Kennywood, West Mifflin, Pennsylvania (412) 461-0500
1. Jack Rabbit, Wood Terrain; Level 2 ★★★
2. Lil' Phantom, Steel Kiddie; Level 1 ★★
3. Phantom's Revenge, Steel Non-looping; Level 4 ★★★★
4. Racer, Wood Dual-track; Level 2 ★★★★
5. Thunderbolt, Wood Terrain; Level 4 ★★★★

Knoebel's Amusement Resort, Elysburg, Pennsylvania (717) 672-2572
1. High Speed Thrill Coaster, Steel Kiddie; Level 3 ★★★★
2. Phoenix, Wood Twister; Level 5 ★★★★★ Super Screamer
3. Twister, Wood Twister; Level 5 ★★★★★ Super Screamer
4. Whirlwind, Steel Looping; Level 3 ★★

Lakemont Park, Altoona, Pennsylvania (814) 949-7275
1. Leap the Dips, Wood Figure Eight; Level 1 ★★★
   (The world's oldest operating roller coaster.)
2. Little Dipper, Steel Kiddie; Level 1 ★★
3. Mad Mouse, Steel Wild Mouse; Level 2 ★★
4. Skyliner, Wood Twister; Level 3 ★★★

Waldameer Park, Erie, Pennsylvania (814) 838-3591
1. Comet Jr., Wood Junior; Level 2 ★★★

Williams Grove, Williams Grove, Pennsylvania (717) 697-8266
1. CYCLONE, Wood Out and Back; Level 4 ★★

South Carolina

Family Kingdom, Myrtle Beach, South Carolina (803) 626-3447
1. SWAMP FOX, Wood Out and Back; Level 3 ★★★★

Pavilion, Myrtle Beach, South Carolina (803) 448-6456
1. HURRICANE, Wood Twister; Level 4 ★★★★
2. LITTLE EAGLE, Steel Junior; Level 1 ★★
3. MAD MOUSE, Steel Wild Mouse; Level 3 ★★★

Tennessee

Dollywood, Pigeon Forge, Tennessee (615) 428-9400
1. BLAZING FURY, Steel Gravity Dark Ride; Level 3 ★★★
2. TENNESSEE TORNADO, Steel Looping; Level 4 ★★★★

Libertyland, Memphis, Tennessee (901) 274-8800
1. REVOLUTION, Steel Looping; Level 3 ★★
2. ZIPPIN PIPPIN, Wood Out and Back; Level 2 ★★★
(This is not only one of the world's oldest operating coasters, it is also the thrill ride of choice of the late Elvis Presley, who used to rent the ride after hours and ride into the night.)

Texas

Sea World of Texas, San Antonio, Texas (210) 523-3000
1. GREAT WHITE, Steel Inverted; Level 5 ★★★★★ Super Screamer
2. STEEL EEL, Steel Non-looping; Level 4 ★★★★

Six Flags Astroworld, Houston, Texas (713) 799-8404
1. BATMAN–THE ESCAPE, Steel Stand-up; Level 5 ★★★★
2. GREEZED LIGHTNIN', Steel Looping Shuttle; Level 4 ★★★★
3. MAYAN MINDBENDER, Enclosed Steel Junior; Level 2 ★★★
4. SERIAL THRILLER, Steel Inverted; Level 5 ★★★★
5. SERPENT, Steel Kiddie; Level 1 ★★
6. TEXAS TORNADO, Steel Looping; Level 5 ★★★★★ Super Screamer
7. TEXAS CYCLONE, Wood Twister; Level 4 ★★★★
8. ULTRA TWISTER, Steel Looping; Level 4 ★★★★
9. VIPER, Steel Looping; Level 3 ★★★★
10. XLR-8, Steel Suspended; Level 2 ★★★

Six Flags Fiesta Texas, San Antonio, Texas (210) 697-5050
1. BOOMERANG, Steel Looping Shuttle; Level 4   ★★★
2. JOKER'S REVENGE, Steel Looping; Level 4   ★★★
3. POLTERGEIST, Steel Looping LIM; Level 5   ★★★★
4. RATTLER, Wood Terrain; Level 3   ★★★
5. ROAD RUNNER EXPRESS, Steel Mine Train; Level 3   ★★★
6. ROLLSCHUHCOASTER, Steel Kiddie; Level 1   ★★★
7. SUPERMAN KRYPTON COASTER, Steel Floorless; Level 4   ★★★★★

Six Flags Over Texas, Arlington, Texas (817) 640-8900
This was the first park built by Six Flags, combining the kind of pleasant family attractions associated with Disney parks with more traditional thrill rides. Six Flags introduced the world to many things that are now commonplace within the theme park industry, such as the log flume, the river rapids ride, the tubular steel roller coaster, Broadway-style entertainment, and the pay-one-price admission plan.
1. BATMAN–THE RIDE, Steel Inverted; Level 5   ★★★★★ Super Screamer
2. FLASHBACK, Steel Looping Shuttle; Level 4   ★★★
3. JUDGE ROY SCREAM, Wood Out and Back; Level 3   ★★★
4. LA VIBORA, Steel Bobsled; Level 2   ★★★
5. MINE TRAIN, Steel Mine Train; Level 2   ★★★★
6. MINI MINE TRAIN, Steel Junior Mine Train; Level 1   ★★★
7. MR. FREEZE, Steel Looping Shuttle LIM; Level 5   ★★★★
8. RUNAWAY MOUNTAIN, Enclosed Steel Junior; Level 3   ★★★
9. SHOCKWAVE, Steel Looping; Level 4   ★★★★★
10. TEXAS GIANT, Wood Twister; Level 5   ★★★★★ Super Screamer
11. TITAN, Steel Non-looping; Level 5   ★★★★
12. WILE E. COYOTE'S GRAND CANYON BLASTER, Steel Kiddie; Level 1   ★★

Wonderland, Amarillo, Texas (806) 383-4712
1. TEXAS TORNADO, Steel Looping; Level 4   ★★★★

Utah

Lagoon, Farmington, Utah (801) 451-0101
1. COLOSSAL FIRE DRAGON, Steel Looping; Level 3   ★★★★
2. JET STAR II, Compact Steel; Level 2   ★★★
3. PUFF THE LITTLE FIRE DRAGON, Steel Kiddie; Level 1   ★★
4. ROLLER COASTER, Wood Out and Back; Level 3   ★★★
5. WILD MOUSE, Steel Wild Mouse; Level 3   ★★★

Judge Roy Scream, Six Flags Over Texas. (Courtesy of Bobby Nagy)

Virginia

Busch Gardens, Williamsburg, Virginia (804) 253-3000
1. ALPENGEIST, Steel Inverted; Level 5 ★★★★★ Super Screamer
2. APOLLO'S CHARIOT, Steel Non-looping; Level 4 ★★★★
3. BIG BAD WOLF, Steel Suspended; Level 3 ★★★★
4. LOCH NESS MONSTER, Steel Looping; Level 4 ★★★★
5. WILDE MAUS, Steel Wild Mouse; Level 2 ★★★★

Paramount's Kings Dominion, Doswell, Virginia (804) 876-5000
1. ANACONDA, Steel Looping; Level 4 ★★★★
2. AVALANCHE, Steel Boblsed; Level 2 ★★★★
3. FLIGHT OF FEAR, Enclosed Steel Looping; Level 5 ★★★★★
4. GRIZZLY, WOOD TWISTER; Level 5 ★★★★★ Super Screamer
5. HURLER, Wood Twister; Level 4 ★★★★
6. HYPERSONIC XLC, Steel Non-looping; Level 4 ★★★★
7. REBEL YELL, Wood Dual-track Out and Back; Level 4 ★★★★
8. RICOCHET, Steel Wild Mouse; Level 3 ★★★★
9. SCOOBY DOO'S GHOSTER COASTER, Wood Junior; Level 2 ★★★
10. SHOCKWAVE, Steel Stand-up; Level 4 ★★★★
11. TAXI JAM, Steel Kiddie; Level 1 ★★★
12. VOLCANO THE BLAST COASTER, Steel Inverted LIM; Level 4 ★★★★

Mr. Freeze, making it chillier at two Six Flags parks. A similar design was used for Batman and Robin—The Chiller. (Courtesy of Six Flags Over Texas)

Washington

Western Washington Fairgrounds, Puyallup, Washington (206) 845-1771
1. ROLLER COASTER, Wood Twister; Level 3   ★★★

West Virginia

Camdon Park, Huntington, West Virginia (304) 429-4231
1. BIG DIPPER, Wood Twister; Level 2   ★★★
2. LIL' DIPPER, Wood Junior; Level 2   ★★★
3. THUNDERBOLT EXPRESS, Steel Looping Shuttle; Level 3   ★★

Wisconsin

Big Chief Kart and Coaster World, Wisconsin Dells, Wisconsin (608) 254-7858
1. CYCLOPS, Wood Terrain; Level 3   ★★★★
2. PEGASUS, Wood Junior; Level 2   ★★★
3. ZEUS, Wood Out and Back; Level 4   ★★★★

SOUTH AMERICA

BRAZIL

Hopi Hari, Vinhedo
1. Katapul, Steel Looping Shuttle; Level 4   ★★★★
2. Montezum, Wood Terrain; Level 4   ★★★★
3. Vurang, Steel Non-looping Enclosed; Level 3   ★★★

Play Centre, São Paolo 11-3618-2700
1. Boomerang, Steel Looping Shuttle; Level 4   ★★★
2. Looping Star, Steel Looping; Level 3   ★★★
3. Tornado, Steel Compact; Level 3   ★★★

Flight of Fear. (Courtesy of Paramount's Kings Dominion)

Terra Encantada, Barra Da Tijuca (021) 2421-9444
1.   MONTE AURORA, Steel Kiddie; Level 1   ★★
2.   MONTE MAKAYA, Steel Looping; Level 5   ★★★★
3.   PIUI, Steel Junior; Level 2   ★★

9 THE BEST ROLLER COASTER TRIPS

Roller coaster fans worldwide have been known to plan entire vacations centered around amusement parks and roller coasters.

Following are some suggested park combinations that will create coaster-oriented vacations lasting anywhere from a long weekend to a week or two. All are flexible and may be added to or shortened to form a trip tailor-made to fulfill your needs.

In most cases, your trip will require hotel stays. Some parks have adjacent hotels; many parks are complete resorts with hotels on the property (these are noted in the trip descriptions). Call the park for information on nearby accommodations.

Many major hotel chains have locations near individual parks. They may be reached by calling the following 800 numbers:

Best Western	1-800-528-1234
Choice Hotels International	1-800-424-6423
(including Sleep Inn, Comfort Inn, Quality Inn, Clarion, and Friendship)	
Days Inn	1-800-325-2525
Econo Lodge	1-800-446-6900
Hilton Hotels	1-800-445-8667
Holiday Inn	1-800-465-4329
Howard Johnson	1-800-654-4329
Hyatt Hotels	1-800-233-1234
Knights Inn	1-800-843-5644
La Quinta	1-800-531-5900
Marriott Hotels	1-800-228-9290

Motel 6	1-800-466-8356
Radisson Hotels	1-800-333-3333
Ramada Inn	1-800-272-6232
Red Roof	1-800-THE-ROOF
Rodeway Inn	1-800-228-2660
Sheraton	1-800-325-3535
Stouffer Hotels	1-800-468-3571
Super 8 Motels	1-800-800-8000

THE WEST COASTER

*Includes Six Flags Magic Mountain, Disneyland,
Knott's Berry Farm and Belmont Park*

Travel Information:

Airport: If flying, use Los Angeles International Airport
Hotel: Southern California is all about driving cars. It is also a major tourist center, with any number of things to do that have nothing to do with theme parks. It is therefore suggested that you center yourself at one hotel for the duration of your stay in Southern California, preferably near the Disneyland Resort area, where hotel rooms and prices are varied and abundant.

Six Flags Magic Mountain, Valencia, California

Located just north of Los Angeles. Take the Magic Mountain exit off I-5. The park is visible from the highway.

Part of the Six Flags California complex (which also includes a great water park known as Six Flags Hurricane Harbor), Six Flags is home to the largest collection of roller coasters in the western United States, including top thrillers X, Superman–The Escape, Riddler's Revenge, and Viper.

During the winter, early spring, and late fall, the park is only open on weekends and holidays.

TIPS FOR THIS PARK: Upon entering the main gate, most guests will head for the Viper or Revolution, located near the entrance, or straight up to the top of Samurai Summit, the location of the awesome Superman–The Escape. Go to the Cyclone Bay area first, near the back left corner of the park, and try riding Psyclone and Déjà Vu first, and work your way around the park in a clockwise pattern. You'll be ahead of the crowds, and by the time you've returned to your starting point, the lines for the coasters nearest the main gate should be shorter.

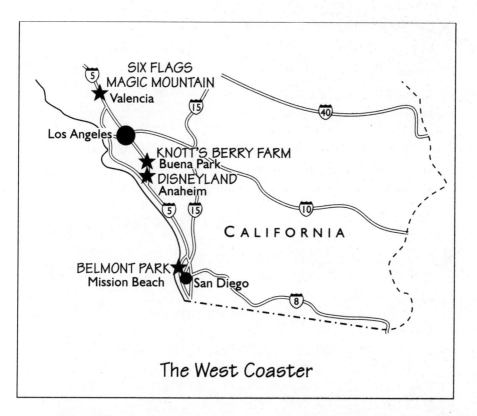

The West Coaster

If you just want to ride the coasters, one day is all it will take (if the park is crowded, that's all you may get to do). If you want to experience all the rest the park has to offer, a two-day visit is recommended.

Knott's Berry Farm, Buena Park, California

In Buena Park, take the Beach Boulevard exit off I-5

Knott's Berry Farm is home to several roller coasters, chief among them Ghost Rider, one of the world's best wooden roller coasters.

TIPS FOR THIS PARK: The park attracts a family crowd, so lines on the more intense coasters are not usually a problem. Go during the week to avoid crowds. A one-day visit should give you your fill, but if you enjoy shows, shopping and the like, you might want to plan accordingly.

Disneyland Resort, Anaheim, California

Take the Disneyland exit off I-5.

The first full-fledged theme park in the world is home to four coasters, all suitable for any member of the family. The adjacent California Adventures is home to California Screamin', a huge steel coaster with a loop that is built to resemble a wooden coaster.

Disneyland is a complete resort, with hotels located directly on the property. It provides a good base location for your West Coaster trip.

~~~~~~

Roller Coaster Fact: Building Big Thunder Mountain Railroad at Disneyland in 1979 cost almost as much as building the entire park back in 1955.

~~~~~~

TIPS FOR THIS PARK: Disneyland gets more visitors than any other park in the country. It's always crowded, but lines move fast. Try going on a day when the park is open until midnight, and get there as soon as the gates open. Head to the Matterhorn first thing, and save Gadget's Go Coaster for the nighttime, when most of the kiddies have gone home.

Belmont Park, San Diego, California
Take I-5 to San Diego. Take the Sea World exit, and follow the road into Mission Beach.

Once a fully operational amusement park, it is now a shopping plaza that includes a classic wooden roller coaster.

TIPS FOR THIS PARK: Since it's not exactly a full amusement park, buy your tickets and ride at your leisure. Be sure to take a stroll on the beach.

VIRGINIA IS FOR ROLLER COASTER LOVERS

Includes Busch Gardens Williamsburg, Paramount's Kings Dominion, and Six Flags America

Travel Information:

Airport: Fly into either Richmond International or Dulles International. *Hotel:* Because the parks are several hours from each other, it is recommended that you book hotels near the parks.

All the parks are easily accessible from I-95, a major East Coast north-south route.

Busch Gardens, Williamsburg, Virginia
Take I-95 to I-295 (in Richmond) to I-64. Exit I-64 at exit 242. Follow signs to route 60, and to the park.

Most major hotel chains have locations throughout the Williamsburg area.

Widely regarded as the most beautiful theme park in the country, this park is themed to old-world European countries.

Roller coasters include the famous Loch Ness Monster, Big Bad Wolf, and Apollo's Chariot.

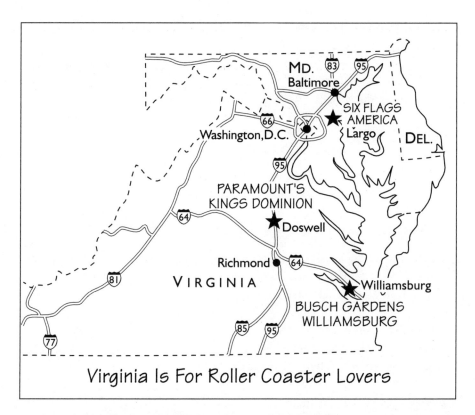

Virginia Is For Roller Coaster Lovers

TIPS FOR THIS PARK: Unless it has no line, bypass Loch Ness Monster, which is right in the front of the park and head back to the themed area known as Oktoberfest, where three of the park's coasters are located. Ride Loch Ness in the afternoon, when lines will be shortest.

Paramount's Kings Dominion, Doswell, Virginia
Located Directly off I-95, at exit 98.

One of the Paramount Parks, and home to four wooden roller coasters and three launched-style steel coasters, the most of either type at any one park in North America.

The Best Western Kings Quarters Hotel is located adjacent to the park, with others throughout the area.

TIPS FOR THIS PARK: Wherever else you head, first hop on the stand-up Shockwave; because of a slow loading process, it always has the most unbearably long and sluggish line in the park. Then head right on back to the Congo section, home to Volcano the Blast Coaster, also a long and slow moving line. At the end of the day, the lines will usually be short on Grizzly, Hurler and Rebel Yell, all three of which absolutely fly at night.

Six Flags America, Largo, Maryland
In Maryland, take exit 15 off I-95/495. Follow Route 214 to the park.

Now part of the Six Flags family of parks, this one features many top-notch thrill rides.

TIPS FOR THIS PARK: While Superman Ride of Steel may be the park's best coaster, try riding Two Face, or the Batwing first thing, as they will have long lines due to lower capacity.

THE EIGHTEEN FLAGS OVER TEXAS TOUR

Includes Six Flags Over Texas, Six Flags Astroworld,
and Six Flags Fiesta Texas

Travel Information:

Airport: Use any of the airports located in the cities containing the parks.
Hotel: Because of the travel time between parks, it is essential to book hotels located near each park.

It is also essential to purchase a Six Flags season pass at whatever park you first attend. The pass will admit you to all three parks, plus any other Six Flags parks you happen upon during your travels.

Six Flags Over Texas, Arlington, Texas
Located midway between Dallas and Forth Worth, off Interstate 30
This park is the first one built by the Six Flags Theme Park Company. It is one of their best and contains one of the world's best wooden roller coasters, among many other high-quality thrillers.

Although there are dozens of hotels and motels throughout the area, the most convenient is the La Quinta Inn, located directly across the street from the park's entrance. Ask for a room with a view of the park; you'll wake up in the morning to the sound of roller coasters rumbling their way through their daily test runs. You'll also be able to walk to the park.

TIPS FOR THIS PARK: Try heading for Flashback and Mr. Freeze first thing, as they are both shuttle style coasters capable of running only one train, and therefore have lower capacity.

Roller Coaster Fact: The Six Flags Over Texas Shock Wave was the first roller coaster to feature two consecutive loops. The loops, each 70 feet high, are positioned next to a freeway running adjacent to the park. For a long time after the ride's debut, the loops were responsible for many car accidents.

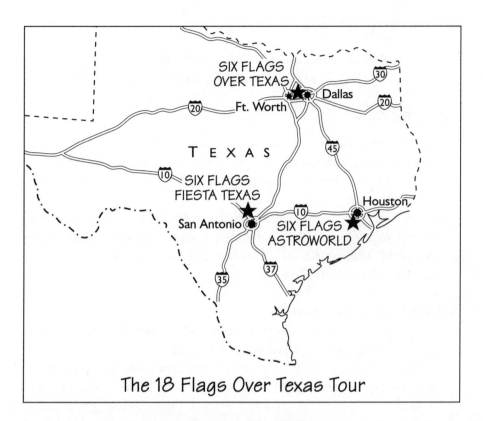

The 18 Flags Over Texas Tour

Six Flags Astroworld, Houston, Texas

Located adjacent to the Astrodome, off the I-610 loop.

After Six Flags built its first three parks, it began buying parks already in existence, starting with this one. It contains the Texas Cyclone, the first copy of the Coney Island Cyclone.

Major hotel chains are located throughout the area. Several are part of the Astro Village, located directly across the street from the parking lot that serves both Six Flags Astroworld and the Astrodome. Call the park for details.

Six Flags Fiesta Texas, San Antonio, Texas

Take Exit 556 off I-10.

Located in an abandoned quarry, the park contains several coasters, which utilize the quarry walls to further their thrills.

Hotels and motels are located throughout the San Antonio metro area.

TIPS FOR THIS PARK: This is a park strong on shows as well as thrill rides, so it attracts a large audience of both family-types and thrill-seekers. Lines can be long, so ride the coasters first thing in the morning and hope for the best.

THE OHIO IS ROLLER COASTER COUNTRY TOUR

*Includes Cedar Point, Six Flags Worlds of Adventure
and Paramount's Kings Island.*

Travel Information:

Airport: While Cedar Point and Six Flags Worlds of Adventure are located near Cleveland, Paramount's Kings Island is just north of Cincinnati. Use either Cleveland Hopkins International or, for a more centrally located airport, Columbus International.

Hotel: Although fine hotels are located near Six Flags, it is probably better to base yourself at a hotel located near Cedar Point when visiting those two parks. A separate hotel is required for Paramount's Kings Island, located about four hours to the south.

Cedar Point, Sandusky, Ohio

Take exit 7 off I-80 (the Ohio Turnpike). Follow route 250 into Sandusky, and follow the clearly marked signs to the park.

Cedar Point is a complete resort located on a Lake Erie peninsula. It contains the greatest collection of roller coasters in the world, a total of fifteen.

Cedar Point has two hotels located on the peninsula, directly adjacent to the amusement park. These, of course, are the most convenient. The park also owns two landside hotels, located near the entrance to the Cedar Point Causeway. Dozens of additional motels are located throughout this resort town. (This author swears by the Maples Motel, 419-626-1575, located directly between the two entrances to the Cedar Point peninsula. It's simple but extremely, comfortable, and it caters to a pleasant clientele, many of whom have been coming back for years. Owners Joan and Ken Faber will look after you like your own mother would).

TIPS FOR THIS PARK: Get to the park early. Lines get extremely long on all the rides, the newest and most popular of which will open well before the scheduled opening time of the park. Try riding Mean Streak first, and work your way to the front of the park. Raptor, located immediately inside the front gate, will have its longest lines first thing in the morning, as

〜〜〜〜〜〜〜〜〜〜〜〜〜〜〜〜〜〜〜〜〜〜〜〜〜〜〜〜〜〜〜〜〜〜〜

Roller Coaster Information: The Corkscrew at Cedar Point was the world's first roller coaster that featured three upside down elements.

〜〜〜〜〜〜〜〜〜〜〜〜〜〜〜〜〜〜〜〜〜〜〜〜〜〜〜〜〜〜〜〜〜〜〜

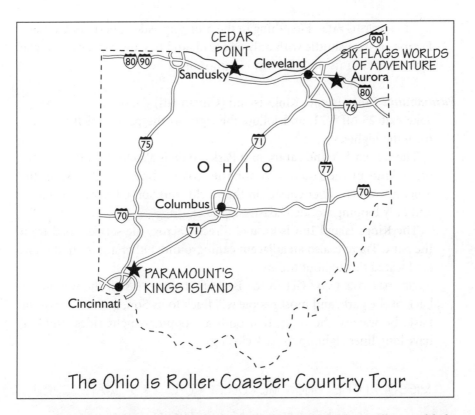

The Ohio Is Roller Coaster Country Tour

will Wicked Twister, a single train shuttle-style ride that will most likely be mobbed all day. One other thing—this park closes its major roller coasters at even the slightest hint of rain. While a few may indeed be operating, it is doubtful that they'll be the ones you came to the park especially to ride. To make matters worse, since this is a resort park, rain does not deter the crowds, either. Plan your visit for a sunny day, if possible during the week in early May or the last week in August, when crowds are at their lightest. Whenever you go, two days are necessary to do everything the park and resort have to offer.

Six Flags Worlds of Adventure, Aurora, Ohio

From I-80, take exit 13 onto I-480. Exit in Twinsburg onto Route 91 north. Take that to Solon, then turn right onto Route 42 to the park, which will be on your left. NOTE: The towns of Solon and Aurora are notorious speed traps! Do not drive even slightly over the posted speed limits, which, by the way, fluctuate greatly and frequently on Route 42 near the park.

Formerly known as Geauga Lake, this classic traditional park is being transformed into a world-class theme park with the addition of not only dozens of new thrill rides and coasters, but with the expansion into the adjacent Sea World of Ohio property, which is now part of the Six Flags park.

TIPS FOR THIS PARK: First thing in the morning, ride Superman Ultimate Escape, as it's a shuttle with only one train and has low capacity, and you won't want to miss it under any circumstances.

Paramount's Kings Island, Kings Island (Cincinnati) Ohio

Take exit 25 off I-71, and follow the signs to the park, which is visible from the highway.

The star park in the Paramount Parks chain is also the best theme park of its kind in the country. Among its coaster lineup is the Beast, the longest wooden roller coaster in the world, and Son Of Beast, the tallest and only looping wooden coaster in the world.

The Kings Island Inn is located directly across the service road from the park. There is also an adjacent campground. Other accommodations are located throughout the area.

TIPS FOR THIS PARK: Get to the Beast first thing. It's all the way in the back of the park, and most people will flock to its Son, in the front of the park. Be warned, however, that both are popular night rides, and will have long lines right up to park closing.

MISSOURI, THE "SHOW ME ROLLER COASTERS" STATE TOUR

Includes Six Flags St. Louis and Worlds of Fun

Travel Information:

Airport: Use either St. Louis International or Kansas City International
Hotel: It's a long drive between the parks. Hotels and motels are located within minutes of each. It is possible, but not recommended, to base yourself out of one hotel for both.

Six Flags St. Louis, Allenton, Missouri

Take Exit 261 off I-44. The park is very visible from the highway.

The latest park actually built by Six Flags, it is also one of its best and most beautiful, situated on a hillside. The world-renowned Screamin' Eagle spans the topmost reaches of the park.

A Ramada Inn is located adjacent to the park and provides shuttle service to the main gate.

TIPS FOR THIS PARK: As soon as the gates open, crowds will either head directly toward Batman–The Ride, located just to the right of the entrance, or the more sprawling Boss to the left. Both dominate the front of the park. Try heading directly up the hill to the Screamin' Eagle, and you'll be able to enjoy it well before everyone else gets up there to it; it will have it's shortest lines both early in the day and just prior to closing.

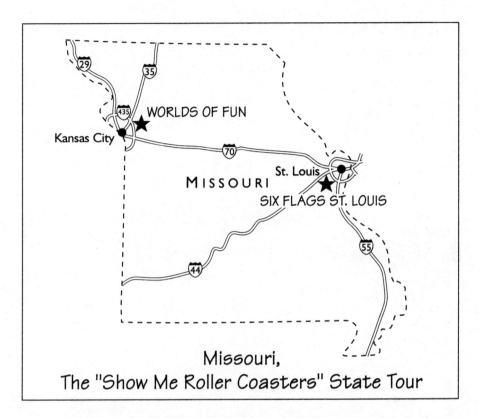

Missouri,
The "Show Me Roller Coasters" State Tour

Worlds of Fun, Kansas City, Missouri

Located off exit 53 on I-435, the park is visible from the highway.

Owned and operated by Cedar Fair, LP, this park is themed after the countries featured in *Around the World in Eighty Days* (although the theming is slowly being relegated to an afterthought). The park is home to three world class roller coasters.

TIPS FOR THIS PARK: Lines here are spread pretty evenly throughout the day, but Boomerang (the most widely sold production-model roller coaster in history), located in the back of the park, will probably have its shortest lines early and late in the day, if you must ride it.

THE KEYSTONE COASTER TOUR

Includes Kennywood, Hersheypark, Knoebels Amusement Resort and
Dorney Park

Travel Information:

Airport: If you wish to be centrally located, fly into Harrisburg International Airport.

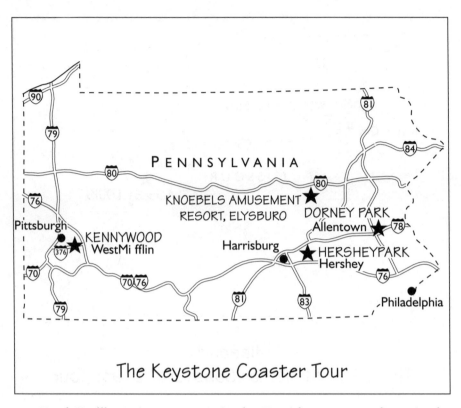

The Keystone Coaster Tour

Hotel: You'll require two—one in the Harrisburg area, and one in the Pittsburgh area.

Kennywood, West Mifflin, Pennsylvania

Take exit 6 off I-76 (The Pennsylvania Turnpike), onto I-376. Take that to exit 9 (Swissvale). From there, it gets a bit complicated, as you'll be driving through residential neighborhoods, but keep a sharp lookout for the bright yellow Kennywood Park arrows, which will point the way. As you cross the Monongahela River, you'll see the park to your left, sitting on top of a bluff overlooking the water.

Kennywood is a fine traditional park, with classic amusement rides next to modern computer-driven thrillers. The park is home to three classic wooden coasters, all originally built in the 1920s, and Phantom's Revenge, a modern steel thriller that at one time was known as Steel Phantom, and was a fierce, looping coaster (the loops have since been removed and replaced with non-inverting trackage).

TIPS FOR THIS PARK: The park tends to begin and end each day with only one-train operations on all its roller coasters. Unless the line is exceptionally short, wait until you can verify that the coaster you want to ride is running at full capacity. Don't be afraid of what appears to be a long line on any of the coasters then, as the waiting times will be surprisingly short.

〰〰〰〰〰〰〰〰〰〰〰〰〰〰〰〰〰〰〰〰〰〰〰

Roller Coaster Fact: Several Roaring Twenties roller coasters have been designated National Historic Landmarks: the Giant Dippers in Santa Cruz and San Diego, California; Jack Rabbit, Racer, and Thunderbolt, at Kennywood (near Pittsburgh, Pennsylvania); Dragon and Kiddie Coasters, at Playland, (Rye, New York); and the Cyclone at Coney Island (Brooklyn, New York).

〰〰〰〰〰〰〰〰〰〰〰〰〰〰〰〰〰〰〰〰〰〰〰

Hersheypark, Hershey, Pennsylvania

Use either exit 27 or 28 off I-81, and follow signs to the park.

This full resort is home to nine coasters, including the Wildcat and Lightning Racer, all patterned after classic 1920s rip-roaring designs.

The Hotel Hershey and Hershey Lodge are located adjacent to the park, with major hotel and motel chains throughout the area.

TIPS FOR THIS PARK: Try heading to the Wildcat and Lightning Racer first thing. On the way, you might also want to hop on the low-capacity Sidewinder if you absolutely need to ride this entirely too-prolific production model. This park gets very crowded with large families. Attempt to schedule your visit for a weekday or Sunday, when crowds tend to be smaller.

Knoebels Amusement Resort, Elysburg, Pennsylvania

Take exit 34 off I-80, onto route 42, take that to route 487. The park is well-hidden, so drive slowly.

The park contains rental cottages, log cabins, and a campground. Motel chains are located near I-80, about fifteen miles from the park.

The best classic amusement park in the United States, Knoebels prides itself on the wonderful atmosphere, food, and setting. A pay-one-price is available on weekdays only, but if the park looks too crowded, don't bother with it—you'll never get on enough rides to make the price worth your while. Instead, opt for the ticket books and the low per-ride prices. Do the park as you see fit, as it has no entrance or exit, and, therefore, also doesn't have any apparent crowd patterns.

Dorney Park, Allentown, Pennsylvania

Take I-78 to exit 16 (if travelling east) or 17 (if travelling west) onto Hamilton Boulevard. The park is visible from the exit.

If you want tall roller coasters, this is the park for you. Dorney is currently home to one of the tallest wood and one of the tallest steel coasters on the East Coast.

TIPS FOR THIS PARK: Because of adjacent water park Wildwater Kingdom, the amusement park section has its smallest crowds all day until early evening. All the rides will get very crowded once the water park closes and the evening crowds arrive. Talon, right in the front of the park, will have long lines all day, but Steel Force, spanning the entire back of the park, should be manageable early in the day.

THE BIG APPLE TOUR

Includes Coney Island's Astroland and Six Flags Great Adventure

Travel Information:

Airport: Use Newark International Airport
Hotel: It is recommended that a hotel in north/central New Jersey should be booked, to not only cut down on room rates, but also as a matter of convenience to both parks.

Coney Island's Astroland, Brooklyn, New York

Take exit 7S off the Belt Parkway, then Ocean Parkway to Surf Avenue.

This is the birthplace of the amusement park, the roller coaster, and every conceivable form of amusement device. It's home to the Cyclone, a National Historic Landmark, as well as the greatest wooden roller coaster in the world.

TIPS FOR THIS PARK: If you want to include the New York Aquarium in your visit to Coney Island, park in the lot adjacent to the Cyclone. The steep parking fee includes an admission ticket to see the fish. Otherwise, park in the Keyspan Stadium lot, or if you plan an early arrival, park at a meter on the street. Bring plenty of quarters with you. The park sells a pay-one-price wristband on non-holiday weekdays only, and was recently named as the nation's best park to go to for more rides with less time waiting in lines.

Six Flags Great Adventure, Jackson, New Jersey

Take exit 7A off the New Jersey Turnpike, or exit 98 from the Garden State Parkway, both of which lead to I-195. Take that to exit 16 (Route 537) and follow the signs.

This is the largest seasonal theme park in the country, with the most rides of any park worldwide, offering some of the best "thrillers" of any

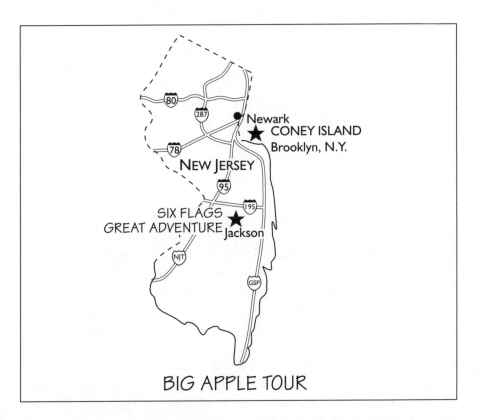

BIG APPLE TOUR

park in the world. The complex also includes a wild animal safari park, and a huge water park, so plan at least two days to see it all.

TIPS FOR THIS PARK: This park has the highest attendance of any seasonal park in the country, so expect big crowds on any weekend throughout the summer. The park does run rides in the rain, so plan to go if the weather is questionable. Once inside the main gate, if you happen to arrive right at park opening, head right to Batman and Robin–The Chiller, as it's a popular attraction, and each track runs only one train each, so the lines will be long all day. Because of a layout that has limited development within the park, the roller coasters are all jammed in at one end of the park or the other and remain crowded right up until park closing.

If time allows, be sure to check out the many amusement piers that dot the New Jersey coastline. They offer an astonishing selection of classic carnival rides and probably the greatest grouping of portable steel coasters in the country. None get crowded during the day, as everyone is usually enjoying the sand and surf of the beaches.

THE LAKE RIVER ESCAPE TOUR

*Includes Lake Compounce, Six Flags New England, and
The Great Escape*

Travel Information:

Airport: Fly into Bradley International, north of Hartford, Connecticut.
Hotel: You'll need two: one near Six Flags New England in Massachusetts
and one near the Great Escape in the Lake George, New York, vicinity.

Lake Compounce, Bristol, Connecticut

Take I-84 to exit 31. Follow signs to Bristol and the park.

Lake Compounce is the oldest operating amusement park in the
United States. It is now owned by the Kennywood Corporation and is
now being constantly upgraded. It's wooden Wildcat dates from 1927
and was completely rebuilt in 1986. The newest kid on the block is
Boulder Dash, an airtime machine that hugs the mountainside within the
park.

TIPS FOR THIS PARK: This is an old park, completely restored and becoming more modern as the days go by rather than the other way around.
The atmosphere is leisurely, and there's plenty for the family to do. Head
straight to Boulder Dash in the back of the park, and make sure you get
some night rides on it before you leave.

Six Flags New England, Agawam, Massachusetts

Take exit 47W off I-91. Take route 190 to route 159. Turn right onto 159,
and follow the road to the park, which will appear on your right as soon
as you have crossed into Massachusetts.

The former Riverside Park is now a member of the Six Flags family,
which means bigger rides, more rides, more to do, and more crowds. Plan
accordingly. The park's Superman Ride of Steel is the world's best roller
coaster, wood or steel.

TIPS FOR THIS PARK: An inconsistent operation makes planning ahead a
bit difficult. Heading to Superman Ride of Steel once inside the gates is a
good idea, but the ride sometimes is not available when the park first
opens. Choose the Cyclone wooden coaster in the north end of the park
instead, if indeed that is open when you arrive. Take advantage of season
pass-holder early entry possibilities.

The Great Escape, Lake George, New York

Take exit 19 off I-87. Go to route 9, turn left, and follow the road to the
park.

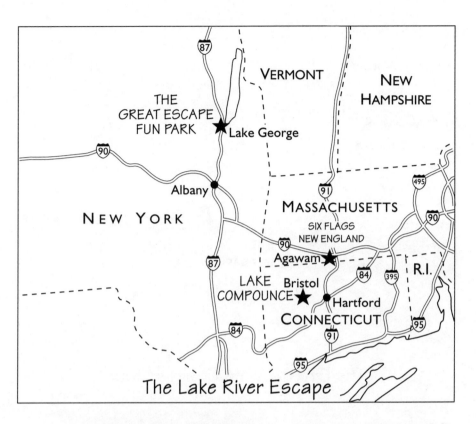

The park began life as Storytown U.S.A. and is now a member of the Six Flags family of theme parks. It is home to the Comet, one of the best roller coasters in the world.

There are dozens of hotels in the Lake George resort area. Several are located directly adjacent to the park.

TIPS FOR THIS PARK: The park's Nightmare roller coaster has one of the slowest moving lines in any park, and you'll wait for hours for this portable steel production model in the dark. Pass on it, or ride it first thing, before the park fills up. The Comet has shorter lines first thing in the morning and late in the day, and *that's* the ride you really came to the park for, right?

THE GREAT LAKES COASTER TOUR

*Includes Sea Breeze, Six Flags Darien Lake and
Paramount Canada's Wonderland*

Travel Information:

Airport: Use Buffalo International Airport.
Hotel: Six Flags Darien Lake, located about midway between the two

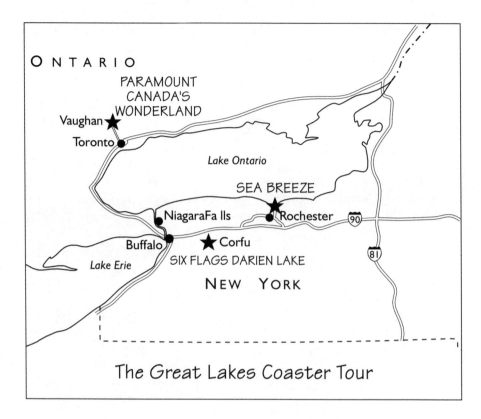

ONTARIO

PARAMOUNT
CANADA'S
WONDERLAND

Vaughan ★

Toronto ●

Lake Ontario

SEA BREEZE ★

NiagaraFa lls ●   ● Rochester   (90)

Buffalo ●   ★ Corfu

Lake Erie   SIX FLAGS DARIEN LAKE   (81)

NEW YORK

The Great Lakes Coaster Tour

other parks, offers RV rentals in its huge campground, which is located adjacent to the amusement park. There is also a full service resort hotel on the premises. Try either of those, or any of the major chain hotels and motels throughout the Buffalo area.

Sea Breeze, Rochester, New York

From I-90, take either exit 45 or 47 onto I-490. Take that to Route 590 (the Sea Breeze Expressway). The park is at the end of the expressway, on Culver Road.

Sea Breeze is a classic traditional park, with several unique coasters and attractions.

TIPS FOR THIS PARK: If possible, do not ride the Jack Rabbit until nighttime. The ride is filled with surprises that work much better in the darkness. Trivia hounds will be interested to know that the steepest drop in the park belongs to the Log Flume, which was purchased and moved from the long-gone Euclid Beach Amusement Park in Cleveland, Ohio.

Six Flags Darien Lake, Corfu, New York

Take the Six Flags Darien Lake exit off I-90, and follow signs to the park.

A combination theme park, water park, and campground resort, SFDL is home to New York State's tallest wood and tallest steel coasters, respectively.

TIPS FOR THIS PARK: The park may get very crowded. If you need to ride the Boomerang production model shuttle, do it first thing. The crowning attraction in the park is Superman Ride of Steel, which will have long lines all day long. Make sure it is running two trains (red and blue) before you attempt to wait on the line.

Paramount Canada's Wonderland, Vaughan, Ontario, Canada

From the United States, take I-90 to I-190 into Canada. Follow the sings to the Queen Elizabeth Way, all the way to Toronto. The park is accessible from either Route 400 or Route 404, just north of Toronto.

You must pass through customs both entering Canada and returning to the United States. Although a passport is not required, it is the best form of identification when traveling to other countries. At the very least, carry your birth certificate and photo ID. Unless you purchase over $500 worth of souvenirs at the park, you do not have to declare them to customs.

Paramount Canada's Wonderland accepts American currency for admission and all purchases. The cash registers will compute the rate of exchange, but please be aware that your change for purchases will be given to you in Canadian currency.

A member of the Paramount Parks chain, the park features the largest collection of roller coasters in Canada, and one of the greatest varieties of coasters in the world.

TIPS FOR THIS PARK: Try to schedule your visit to this park during a weekday on what is a holiday in the United States that is not celebrated in Canada (for example, Memorial Day and Independence Day). The park can get extremely busy on weekends and Canadian holidays. Most of the park's coasters line the back of the park; start with the Mighty Canadian Minebuster and work your way clockwise. Ride the inverted Top Gun during midday, since it is located next to the entrance and will have its shortest lines at that time.

10 THE TOP FIVE ROLLER COASTER LISTS

Now that you're really a diehard fan of roller coasters, simple top ten lists just won't do anymore. True lovers of roller coasters go beyond listing the best wood or steel rides, compiling data in even the most obscure coaster categories—like these:

BEST INVERTED COASTERS

1. ALPENGEIST, Busch Gardens, Williamsburg, Virginia
    Built over and through a ravine, with some amazing visuals for both riders and spectators. The sheer power of this ride and size of its elements are truly amazing.

2. RAPTOR, Cedar Point, Sandusky, Ohio
    A big ride with some amazing nuances, all dictated by having to squeeze into tight spaces and build around existing structures.

3. MONTU, Busch Gardens, Tampa, Florida
    It's the natural evolution of the inverted roller coaster—all the best of every ride of this type is rolled into this one.

4. Batman–The Ride,
    Six Flags Great America, Gurnee, Illinois
    Six Flags Great Adventure, Jackson, New Jersey
    Six Flags Magic Mountain, Valencia, California
    Six Flags St. Louis, Allenton, Missouri
    Six Flags Over Georgia, Atlanta, Georgia
    Six Flags Over Texas, Arlington, Texas

Alpengeist, Busch Gardens, Williamsburg. (Courtesy of Busch Gardens)

〜〜〜〜〜〜〜〜〜〜〜〜〜〜〜〜〜〜〜〜〜〜〜〜〜〜〜

Roller Coaster Fact: Only one roller coaster at a time can hold the title of the best coaster in the world, but since the 1960s (when this type of rating first became prominent), many have held the position. Among the coasters to hold the top title are the Cyclone, Coney Island; Thunderbolt, Kennywood; Beast, Paramount's Kings Island; Texas Cyclone, Six Flags Astroworld; Riverside Cyclone, Riverside Park; Timber Wolf, Worlds of Fun; Magnum XL-200, Cedar Point; and Texas Giant, Six Flags Over Texas.

〜〜〜〜〜〜〜〜〜〜〜〜〜〜〜〜〜〜〜〜〜〜〜〜〜〜〜

Identical thrill machines, with the Missouri version a mirror image of the other five. Compact and relentless.

5. VOLCANO THE BLAST COASTER, Paramount's Kings Dominion, Doswell, Virginia
Utilizing LIMs to launch the train, once out of the station, and once into a mountain, which provides the train the ability to appear as a lava blast out of its top, this is the world's fastest inverted. There's not much to the design, and it's over just when it looks like something's beginning, but it's fast, smooth, and does provide thrills.

FIVE BEST STAND-UP COASTERS

1. MANTIS, Cedar Point, Sandusky, Ohio
A super-intense experience, with lightning quick elements, a demented layout, and a beautiful setting, partially over a lake.

2. RIDDLER'S REVENGE, Six Flags Magic Mountain, Valencia, California
Themed to the Batman motion picture series, this green gargantua flips riders every which way but loose.

3. CHANG, Six Flags Kentucky Kingdom, Louisville, Kentucky
Almost a copy of Mantis, but slightly larger and adding one more inversion in place of Mantis's spaghetti-bowl figure-eight finale.

Opposite Page: Cedar Point's Mantis, an example of a stand-up coaster. (Courtesy of Dan Feicht, Cedar Point)

〜〜〜〜〜〜〜〜〜〜〜〜〜〜〜〜〜〜〜〜〜〜〜〜〜〜〜〜〜〜〜〜〜〜〜〜

Roller Coaster Fact: The five tallest looping roller coasters in the world: Manhattan Express (203 feet), New York New York Resort and Casino, Las Vegas, Nevada; Alpengeist (195 feet), Busch Gardens, Williamsburg, Virginia; Viper (188 feet), Six Flags Magic Mountain, Valencia, California; Great American Scream Machine (173 feet), Six Flags Great Adventure, Jackson, New Jersey; Shock Wave (170 feet), Six Flags Great America, Gurnee, Illinois.

〜〜〜〜〜〜〜〜〜〜〜〜〜〜〜〜〜〜〜〜〜〜〜〜〜〜〜〜〜〜〜〜〜〜〜〜

4.   VORTEX, Paramount's Great America, Santa Clara, California
Very enjoyable ride with a twisting double dip that literally lifts you off your feet.

5.   IRON WOLF, Six Flags Great America, Gurnee, Illinois
Wild layout, with a figure-eight finale featuring many sudden changes of direction.

FIVE BEST MINE TRAINS

1.   BIG THUNDER MOUNTAIN RAILROAD, The Magic Kingdon at Walt Disney World, Orlando, Florida
The perfect example of what this type of ride should be, heavily themed throughout in true Disney fashion.

2.   ADVENTURE EXPRESS, Paramount's Kings Island, Cincinnati, Ohio
Special-effects-laden terrain ride with unexpected drops and hidden turns.

3.   RUNAWAY TRAIN, Six Flags Over Texas, Arlington, Texas
The world's first-ever mine train roller coaster still has what it takes. Hidden tunnels and truly inspired twisting, dropping trackage.

4.   THUNDERATION, Silver Dollar City, Branson, Missouri
The world's fastest mine-train-type attraction. Using the park's natural terrain, the ride gets going right out of the station and doesn't have a lift-hill until the very end, which leads into a perilous final drop, the longest on a mine train. Several seats on the ride face backward.

5.   ROAD RUNNER EXPRESS, Six Flags Fiesta Texas, San Antonio, Texas
Built on the side of a natural rock quarry that the park is situated in, this is a fun, fast family ride with the appropriate thrills for a ride of its kind.

Children of all ages thrill to the charms of Walt Disney World's Big Thunder Mountain Railroad, rated best mine train. (Courtesy of Walt Disney World)

Roller Coaster Fact: The Cyclone Racer at the Pike in Long Beach, California (dismantled iin 1968) was the first roller coaster movie star. It made appearances in *The Beast From 20,000 Fathoms, Strike Me Pink,* Abbott and Costello's *The Dancing Masters,* and *It's A Mad, Mad, Mad, Mad World,* among others.

FIVE BEST ENCLOSED COASTERS

1. ROCK AND ROLLER COASTER, Disney-MGM Studios at Walt Disney World, Orlando, Florida
    Disney's first-ever USA looping coaster, in the dark and accompanied by Aerosmith tunes from speakers built right into the trains. Smooth, fast and unpredictable.

2. SPACE MOUNTAIN, Disneyland, Anaheim, California
    Very different from the Florida version, this one has similar theming but with a much more dynamic layout, with wilder turns and sudden drops.

3. FLIGHT OF FEAR,
    Paramount's Kings Dominion, Doswell, Virginia
    Paramount's Kings Island, Cincinnati, Ohio

    Identical attractions with amazing theming and tight twisting layouts. These rides feature four inversions. Of more special note, they are the first full-circuit roller coasters to use a linear induction launch system. Instead of rolling casually out of the staton onto a lift hill, the trains catapult from 0 to 60 mph into an interior lit by strobes and multicolored spotlights.

4. SPACE MOUNTAIN, Disneyland Paris, Marne La Vallee, France
    While it's theming is similar to Disney's USA Space Mountains, this one has a long, more traditional coaster train rocketing up a lift-hill into a real upside down roller coaster.

5. SPACE MOUNTAIN, The Magic Kingdom, Walt Disney World, Orlando, Florida
    The original, and predecessor to it's Disneyland cousin. A dual-tracked ride (one side's a mirror image of the other) with toboggan-style seating. Although Disney has never made the comparison, this ride is extremely similar in setup and layout to the world's original steel coaster, Disneyland's Matterhorn.

The Beast, Paramount's Kings Island. (Courtesy of Paramount's Kings Island)

BEST WOODEN TERRAIN COASTERS

1. LEGEND, Holiday World, Santa Claus, Indiana
    A bigger brother to the park's other classic, Raven, providing about the same type of ride, but in *much* greater quantities.

2. BOSS, Six Flags St. Louis, Allenton, Missouri
    This is a ride that combines terrain and elements of both a twister and out and back to greatest effect. A 150-foot-long double dip is just the beginning of this ferocious ride.

3. RAVEN, Holiday World, Santa Claus, Indiana
    The smaller upstart in the Holiday World family, this ride features sudden drops and tight turns as its stand-out features. It doesn't have the sheer power of larger rides of its type, but doesn't only rely on terrain like others do to provide the thrills.

4. BEAST, Paramount's Kings Island, Cincinnati, Ohio
    The granddaddy of all terrain coasters, this is also the longest wooden roller coaster in the world. Two lift-hills lead into a fast trp over thirty-five acres of wooded, rolling land in the back of the park. You can't see much of this ride from any vantage point in or out of the park; therefore, its many pleasures remain a mystery to first-time riders.

~~~~~~

Roller Coaster Fact: The five longest wooden roller coaster drops in the world: Son of Beast (214 feet), Paramount's Kings Island, Cincinnati, OH; Colossus (169 feet), Heide Park, Soltau, Germany Hercules (157 feet), Dorney Park, Allentown, Pennsylvania; Mean Streak (155 feet), Cedar Point, Sandusky, Ohio; Boss (150 feet), Six Flags, St. Louis, Allenton, Missouri American Eagle (147 feet), Six Flags Great America, Gurnee, Illinois; Beast (141 feet), Paramount's Kings Island, Cincinnati, Ohio.

~~~~~~

5.   BOULDER DASH, Lake Compounce, Bristol, Connecticut
The world's only roller coaster built entirely on the side of a mountain, it probably could have used the terrain much more to its advantage in providing some good solid drops. What it does instead is serve up (without even one heart-pounding drop) direction changes, airtime-laden hops, and a fast, furious trip that just comes *this* close to being a great ride.

BEST SUSPENDED COASTERS

1.   TOP GUN, Paramount's Kings Island, Cincinnati, Ohio
A brief but extremely intense experience. Spanning a ravine, the swinging cars fly through the course with abandonment, and you'll be convinced that collision with a support post is imminent. Doesn't even come close to giving you a moment to catch your breath.

2.   NINJA, Six Flags Magic Mountain, Valencia, California
This ride's hightest point is on top of the mini-mountain in the center of this park. Form there, it's non-stop as the layout winds down one side of the mountain—above walkways and entangled with other rides—with the cars swinging at times to 10 degrees above horizontal.

3.   BIG BAD WOLF, Bushc Gardens, Williamsburg, Virginia
The world's first successful suspended roller coaster. Heavily themed throughout the course, with trains traveling through a village, which leads to the grand finale—a large drop into an S-turn over water. One of the best-loved roller coasters in the world.

4.   FORTRESS OF EAGLE, Everland, Seoul, Korea
The tallest suspended roller coaster in the world, this ride also utilizes natural terrain to provide a stunning array of large drops and high-speed twisting turns.

Top Gun, Paramount's Kings Island. (Courtesy of Paramount's Kings Island)

5. VORTEX, Paramount Canada's Wonderland, Vaughan, Ontario, Canada
    A twiin of the aforementioned Top Gun (this one came first). Vortex begins on a man-made-mountain and ends over a lake.

FIVE BEST STEEL MEGA-COASTERS

1. SUPERMAN RIDE OF STEEL, Six Flags New England, Agawam, Massachusetts
    There is no other ride in the world that compares to the experience of this one, probably the ultimate in thrill riding.

2. MAGNUM XL-200, Cedar Point, Sandusky, Ohio
    The first full-circuit roller coaster ever to stretch over 200 feet high, this masterpiece still hasn't been topped in its ability to provide good, solid raw thrills.

3. NITRO, Six Flags Great Adventure, Jackson, New Jersey
    A great ride that combines the direction changes of a twister with the airtime and hills of an out and back to fullest advantage. Nitro's first drop may be one of the best in the business.

4.   STEEL FORCE, Dorney Park, Allentown, Pennsylvania
Similar to Magnum in layout and pacing, this one features a first drop into an underground tunnel, an amazing helix, and a stunning finale of air-time-filled rabbit hops.

5.   MILLENNIUM FORCE, Cedar Point, Sandusky, Ohio
The first full-circuit coaster to reach over 300 feet, this powerful monster is all about high-speed, direction changes, and exhilaration.

FIVE BEST AIRTIME WOODEN COASTERS

1.   BOULDER DASH, Lake Compounce, Bristol, Connecticut
This mountainside terrain ride is an out and back, but provides more twists and turns than most twisters. It also provides over a dozen moments of airtime, many during a jog to the left or right that moves the rider laterally as well.

2.   COMET, The Great Escape, Lake George, New York
It is impossible to remain totally seated during this ride. In fact, there are more moments of negative gravity on this ride than the ride itself has hills to provide them.

3.   HURLER, Paramount's Carowinds, Charlotte, North Carolina
Paramount's Kings Dominion, Doswell, Virginia
A rare pair of identical wooden roller coasters, each with large first drops leading into a series of low hills, each providing amazingly orchestrated floating negative g's.

4.   BIG DIPPER, Six Flags Worlds of Adventure, Aurora, Ohio
This 1920's claissc is the way roller coasters used to be. It doesn't have great height, although it was the world's *longest* roller coaster when it was built. Each hill either lifts or throws you out of your seat, and several bends in the track seize the moment you're flying to throw you to the side as well.

5.   THUNDER RUN, Six Flags Kentucky Kingdom, Louisville, Kentucky
This is the original desing that the Paramount Hurlers were based on. It has the same moments of negative gravity as the previously mentioned pair, but on this ride, passengers don't "float" out of the seat—they get *launched* out.

FIVE BEST FIRST DROPS

1. MILLENNIUM FORCE, Cedar Point, Sandusky, Ohio
   The tallest full-circuit roller coaster in the United States, the 300-foot, 80-degree drop that begins this ride of speed also provides the best free-falling sensation of any coaster in the country.

2. SUPERMAN RIDE OF STEEL, Six Flags New England, Agawam, Massachusetts
   At 80 feet shorter than Millennium Force, but of similar steepness, this one dives into an underground tunnel filled with fog, which heightens the feeling of being flung into an abyss.

3. NITRO, Six Flags Great Adventure, Jackson, New Jersey
   While not as steep as some of the newer breed of steel coasters, this one, at 66 degrees on a 215-foot drop is exquisitely shaped to make riders feel they are curling under the track as they dive.

4. CYCLONE, Coney Island's Astroland, Brooklyn, New York
   A dwarf in a land of giants, but at 85 feet, it proves that a drop need not be 200 feet to provide a bone-chilling thrill. Still feels much higher than it actually is.

Millennium Force, Cedar Point, the first full-circuit coaster to top the 300 foot mark. (Dan Feicht, Cedar Point)

~~~~~~

Roller Coaster Fact: Charles Lindbergh is quoted as saying that a ride on the Coney Island Cyclone was more excitiing than a transatlantic flight.

~~~~~~

5. STEEL FORCE, Dorney Park, Allentown, Pennsylvania
Feels remarkably steep and force-filled, and dives into an underground tunnel that appears, from 205 feet above, as if it's too small for the train to fit.

FIVE BEST FINISHES

1. SUPERMAN RIDE OF STEEL, Six Flags New England, Agawam, Massachusetts
After a swirling, diving figure-eight section, the train heads for a series of in-line rabbit hops that provide massive airtime, after which the train dives to the right and literally stops on a dime.

2. TEXAS GIANT, Six Flags Over Texas, Arlington, Texas
Over the first two-thirds of this ride, you get large, twisting drops, and sudden changes of direction. Nearing the finish, the trains suddenly pick up speed on track that dives into the dense wooden structure of the ride, enveloping riders within walls of timber, as the track wraps around the entire main structure on a series of small hops taken at breathless speed.

3. MAGNUM XL-200, Cedar Point, Sandusky, Ohio
A relentless series of rabbit hops, all providing slammer airtime, and so relentless that until the ride comes to a complete stop, passengers don't even have time to relax.

4. RAVEN, Holiday World, Santa Claus, Indiana
More than halfway through the course, a large drop plunges passengers into a valley. The track veers to avoid a tree here and there, and the coaster roars to a finish on a large banked turn, twisting to the left into the station.

5. BIG BAD WOLF, Bush Gardens, Williamsburg, Virginia
The first half of the ride is swift and playful. A second lift-hill carries passengers to the highest point, before dropping them down a hillside to a river, then into a wickedly twisted S-turn.

FIVE BEST TUNNELS

1. BEAST, Paramount's Kings Island, Cincinnati, Ohio
Some roller coasters are lucky to have one tunnel, if any at all. This one has three. The best are the first one, and underground burrow that the first drop plunges into, and the last, which partially encloses the 540-degree helix that makes up the finale.

2. SUPERMAN RIDE OF STEEL, Six Flags New England, Agawam, Massachusetts
There are two fiendish tunnels on this ride. The first, at the base of the first drop, is long and flat, and it feels as if the train will never emerge from the darkness. The second, coming near ride's end, is a surprise and dives under a walkway. Both tunnels are filled with fog, enhancing the floating effect inside.

3. GRIZZLY, Paramount's Kings Dominion, Doswell, Virginia
It's brief, but is totally hidden, and comes at a moment immediately after passengers have been launched off their seats in an exquisite moment of airtime. Look out! The tunnel looks too small to allow the train to fit into it, and it contains a whopping surprise!

4. MAGNUM XL 200, Cedar Point, Sandusky, Ohio
While the train is going far too fast to appreciate the blackness of the three tunnels on this ride, they contain either total darkness, or lights and music effects with fog, and are very effective.

5. FLYER COMET, Whalom Park, Lunenburg, Massachusetts
This classic wooden ride has been around since the 1940's. The tunnel, dubbed the "black hole", was added in the 1990's. It's an extremely dark, long exercise in terror, and features several surprises.

FIVE MOST BEAUTIFUL ROLLER COASTERS

(All wood coasters, incidentally)

1. MEAN STREAK, Cedar Point, Sandusky, Ohio
By night, this isn't just a roller coaster. It's a pile of gold, sculpted to resemble a roller coaster. By day, just as impressive; the dense structure is overpowering, and is designed with true symmetry. The queue line is totally

Mean Streak, Cedar Point. (Courtesy of Dan Feicht, Cedar Point)

within the structure, and passengers waiting to ride will feel insignificant as they stand surrounded by these huge walls of wooden lattice work.

2.   SCREAMIN' EAGLE, Six Flags St. Louis, Allentown, Missouri
      The park sits on a hillside, and traveling about halfway up the slope. At the park's highest point sits this gorgeous white, wooden structure, a classic out-and-back design that runs the entire length of the park. Truly a masterpiece of roller coaster design as art.

3.   GREAT AMERICAN SCREAM MACHINE, Six Flags Over Georgia, Atlanta, Georgia

Roller coasters are thrilling to ride, but if they happen to be designed like Atlanta's Great American Scream Machine, they are also beautiful sculptures. (Courtesy of Bobby Nagy)

Another breathtaking example of coaster sculpture. Beautiful lines, fluid curves, and partially reflected in a lake.

4.   GIANT DIPPER, Santa Cruz Beach Boardwalk, Santa Cruz, California
     Sensuously curving and dipping, this classic 1924 ride contrasts a stark, white structure with bright red track.

5.   WILDCAT, Hersheypark, Hershey, Pennsylvania
     Gorgeous curve after curve after curve. There is not one piece of this structure that couldn't be described as graceful. Has many of the delicacies usually found only in a superbly detailed hand-made doily.

Glossary

Airtime: The sensation of lifting out of your seat when a roller coaster goes down or over a hill. Since you, the passenger, are lighter than the train, you become "weightless" at this moment.

Camel Back: A roller coaster hill—usually a tall one—that travels in a straight line as it goes up, over, then down.

Clothoid Loop: A 360-degree upside-down loop shaped like a teardrop.

Element: An individual part of a roller coaster's design, such as a hill, loop, turn, etc.

Fan Turn: A horseshoe-shaped turn, usually found on wooden coasters, with its highest point at the center of the turn.

Heartline Spiral: A forward-moving, in-line inversion, which turns in a barrel-roll motion, so the rider's center of gravity shifts to the heart.

Hypercoaster: Any coaster over 200 feet tall.

Linear Induction Motor (LIM): A new bread of coaster-launching mechanism, using motors that create an electromagnetic current to propel the train. This allows for faster speeds without the need for high hills.

Rabbit Hop: the name given to the smaller roller coaster hills, widely known to provide the passenger with airtime.

Spaghetti Bowl: Tight, twisting coaster track, usually confined to a small area, difficult to follow and wild in nature.

Spiral Drop: the type of roller coaster drop that turns—sometimes a full 180 degrees—while steeply diving to the ground.

Station Air Gates: Operated using hydraulic pressure, these are the gates used to keep passengers from the track area until the time that it is safe to board the coaster train.

Transfer Track: A section of track on all coasters that mechanically moves to and from the main track, facilitating the addition or removal of trains from the circuit.

Trick-Track: A section of track with one side higher than the other, rapidly alternating, which pitches the coaster car (and passenger) from one side to the other.

Vertical Spread: A term applied to roller coasters built in ravines or other such uneven types of terrain, specifically to the height measurement from the highest point of the coaster on the highest part of the ground to the lowest point of the coaster on the lowest part of the ground.

Index

NOTE: *italic page numbers* indicate picture; **bold page numbers** indicate "Best of"

Acme Gravity Powered Roller Ride (Six Flags St. Louis), 84
Adventure Express (Paramount's Kings Island), 90, **124**
Adventureland: Iowa, 82; New York, 87
Alabama, 75; Visionland, **45**, 75
Allen, John, 9, 11, 15, 23
Alpengeist (Busch Gardens), 25, **49**, 97, **120**, *121*, 124
Alpine Bobsled (Great Escape), 88
Americana Amusement Park (OH), 89
American Eagle (Six Flags Great America), 81
Anaconda (Paramount's Kings Dominion), 97
Ant Farm Express (Wild Adventures), 81
Apollo's Chariot (Busch Gardens), 25, 97
Arkansas Twister (Magic Springs), 75
Arnold's Park (IA), 82
Arrow Dynamics, 16–18, 29
Australia, 65–66
Avalanche (Paramount's Kings Dominion), 16, 97

Baker, Harry, 15–16
Bartlett, Norman, 15
Bat (Paramount Canada's Wonderland), 74
Batman and Robin—the Chiller (Six Flags Great Adventure), **49**, 59, 60, 87, *87*, 115
Batman Knight Flight (Six Flags Worlds of Adventure), **49**, 91
Batman—The Dark Night (Six Flags New England), 83
Batman—The Escape (Six Flags Astroworld), 95
Batman—The Ride (Six Flags), 50, **50**, **120**; Great Adventure, 87; Great America, *24*, 25, 81; Magic Mountain, 76; New

England, 83; Over Georgia, 80; Over Texas, 96; St. Louis, 84
Batwing (Six Flags America), 83
Bear Trax (Sea Breeze), 88
Beast (Paramount's Kings Island), 58, 90, 110, *127*, **133**; facts about, 43, 128, history of, 11, 16, 21, *22*
Beastie (Paramount's Kings Island), 90
Bell's Amusement Park (OK), 91
Belmont Park (CA), 7, 16, 75, 104
Big Apple (Coney Island), 87
Big Bad John (Magic Springs), 75
Big Bad Wolf (Busch Gardens), 11, 17, 97, **128**, **132**
Big Chief Kart and Coaster World (WI), 98
Big Dipper: Camden Park, 98; Six Flags Worlds of Adventure, 6, 60, 91, **130**
Big Thunder Mountain Railroad: Disneyland, 75, 104; Disney World, 80, **124**, *125*
Bill, Larry, 25–26
Blackbeard's Lost Treasure Train (Six Flags Great Adventure), 87
Blackpool Pleasure Beach (England), 57, 58, 69, 70
Blazing Fury (Dollywood), 95
Blue Streak: Cedar Point, 90; Conneaut Lake Park, 92
Bolliger, Walter, 25
Boodley, Mike, 27, 29
Boomerang, 29; Great Escape, 88; Knott's Berry Farm, 76; La Ronde, 74; Six Flags Darien Lake, 88, 119; Six Flags Elitch Gardens, 78; Six Flags Fiesta Texas, 96; Six Flags Marine World, 77; Wild Adventures, 81; Worlds of Fun, 84, 111
Boss (Six Flags St. Louis), 42, 84, **127**, 128
Boulder Dash (Lake Compounce), 42, 78, 116, **128**, **130**
Brainstormer (Disney World), 80
Brain Teaser (Six Flags Darien Lake), 88

Buffalo Bill's Resort and Casino (NV), 84
Bug Out (Wild Adventures), 81
Busch Gardens (FL), 79; Kumba, 25, **51**, 79, *79*; Montu, 25, **53**, 79, **120**
Busch Gardens (VA), 97, 104–5; Alpengeist, 25, **49**, 97, **120**, *121*, 124; Big Bad Wolf, 11, 17, 97, **128**, **132**

California, 75–77, 102–4; history of coasters, 7, 8, 9, 16. *See also* Knott's Berry Farm; Six Flags Magic Mountain
California Screamin' (Disney's California Adventure), 75, 103
Camden Park (WV), 98
Canada, 73–74, 119
Cannon Ball (Lake Winnepesaukah), 80
Cannonball (Waterville USA), 75
Canobie Lake Park (NH), 85
Canyon Blaster: Grand Slam Canyon, 84; Six Flags Magic Mountain, 76
Capital Express (Les Galleries Capitale), 74
Carolina Cyclone (Paramount's Carowinds), 89
Carolina Gold Rusher (Paramount's Carowinds), 89
Casino Pier (NJ), 86
Castles and Coasters (AZ), 75
Cedar Creek Mine Ride (Cedar Point), 90
Cedar Point (OH), 17–18, **56–57**, *57*, 89–90, 108–9; Mantis, 90, **122**, *123*; Mean Streak, 90, 108, 128, **133–34**, *134*; Millennium Force, 12, **52**, 90, **130**, *131*, 131; Raptor, 25, **54**, 90, 108, **120**. *See also* Magnum XL-200
Chang (Six Flags Kentucky Kingdom), 82, **122**
Cheetah (Wild Adventures), 81
China, 62
Church, Fred, 6–7, 16, 27, 46
Clementon Lake Park (NJ), 86
Cobb, William (William Cobb and Associates), 23–24, 43
Cobra: La Ronde, 74; Six Flags Marine World, 77
Colorado, 47, 78
Colossal Fire Dragon (Lagoon), 96
Colossus (Six Flags Magic Mountain), 76
Comet: Great Escape, 13–14, **43**, 88, *89*, 117, **130**; Hersheypark, 92; Stricker's Grove, 91
Comet Jr. (Waldameer Park), 94
Coney Island (NY), 3, 4–5, 6, 87, 114; Cyclone, *3*, 8, *9*, 14, 16, 23, **41**, 43–44, 47, 87, 88, 113, 114, **131**, 132
Conneaut Lake Park (PA), 92
Connecticut, 78, 116. *See also* Lake Compounce
Corkscrew: Cedar Point, 90, 108; Michigan's Adventure, 83; Playland (Canada), 73; Valleyfair, 84
Cornball Express (Indiana Beach), 82

Custom Coasters International (CCI), 25–26
Cyclone, 7, 14, 16; Coney Island, *3*, 8, *9*, 14, 16, 23, **41**, 43–44, 47, 87, 88, 113, 114, **131**, 132; Lakeside Amusement Park, 78, *78*; Six Flags New England, **43**, 83, 116; Six Flags Over Georgia, 14, 22–23, **43–44**, 80; Williams Grove, 95
Cyclops (Big Chief Kart and Coaster World), 98

Dahlonega Mine Train (Six Flags Over Georgia), 80
Dauphinee, Bill, 15
Déjà Vu (Six Flags): Great America, 81; Magic Mountain, 76; Over Georgia, 80
Demon: Paramount's Great America, 76; Six Flags Great America, 81
Desert Storm (Castles and Coasters), 75
Desperado (Buffalo Bill's Resort and Casino), 18, 84
Diamond Back (Frontier City), 91
Diamond Mine Run (Magic Springs), 75
Dinn, Charles (Dinn Corporation), 21–23, 25
Disaster Transport (Cedar Point), 90
Disneyland (CA), 8, 9, 75, 103–4; Matterhorn, 9, 16, 41, 75
Disneyland Paris (France), 67, **126**
Disney-MGM Studios (FL), 79, **126**
Disney's Animal Kingdom (FL), 80
Disney's California Adventure (CA), 75
Disney World (FL), 79–80; Big Thunder Mountain Railroad, 80, **124**, *125*; Space Mountain, 80, **126**
Dollywood (TN), 95
Dorney Park (PA), 92, 113–14; Steel Force, 30, *39*, **54**, 92, **130**, **132**
Double Loop (Six Flags Worlds of Adventure), 91
Do Wopper (Morey's Piers), 86
Dragon: Adventureland, 82; La Ronde, 74
Dragon Coaster (Playland), 16, **88**, 113
Dragon Frye (Paramount Canada's Wonderland), 74
Dueling Dragons (Islands of Adventure), 80
Dutch Wonderland (PA), 92

Elitch Gardens (CO), 47, 78
Enchanted Forest (OR), 91
England, 69–71. *See also* Blackpool Pleasure Beach
Europe, 66–72
Excalibur (Valleyfair), 84
Expedition Geforce (Germany), **50**, 68

Face/Off (Paramount's Kings Island), 90
Family Flyer (Playland), 88
Family Kingdom (SC), 95
Fire in the Hole (Silver Dollar City), 84

Flashback (Six Flags): Magic Mountain, 76; New England, 83; Over Texas, 96
Flight of Fear (Paramount): Kings Dominion, 97, *99*, **126**; Kings Island, 90, **126**
Flitzer: Morey's Piers, 86; Playland, 86
Florida, 79–80. *See also* Busch Gardens; Disney World
Flyer Comet (Whalom Park), **133**
Flying Coaster (Six Flags Elitch Gardens), 78
Flying Super Saturator (Paramount's Carowinds), 89
Flying Unicorn (Islands of Adventure), 80
Fortress of Eagle (South Korea), 65, **128**
Frontier City (OK), 91
Funtown USA (ME), 83

Gadget's Go Coasters (Disneyland), 75
Galaxie: Canobie Lake Park, 85; Indiana Beach, 82
Geauga Lake (OH). *See* Six Flags Worlds of Adventure
Gemini (Cedar Point), 56, 90
Georgia, 80–81. *See also* Six Flags Over Georgia
Georgia Cyclone, 14, 22–23, **43–44**, 80
Georgia Scorcher (Six Flags Over Georgia), 80
Ghost Rider (Knott's Berry Farm), **44**, 76
Ghost Town in the Sky (NC), 89
Giant Coaster (Arnolds Park), 82
Giant Dipper: Belmont Park, 7, 16, 75, 113; Santa Cruz Beach Boardwalk, 76, *77*, 113, **135**
Golden Nugget Mine Ride (Morey's Piers), 86
Gold Rush (Wild Adventures), 81
Gold Rusher (Six Flags Magic Mountain), 76
Goliath (Six Flags Magic Mountain), 76
Goliath, Jr. (Six Flags Magic Mountain), 77
Grand Slam Canyon (NV), 84
Gravity Defying Corkscrew (Silverwood), 16, 81
Gravity Pleasure Road (Coney Island, NY), 5
Greased Lightnin' (Paramount's Great America), 76
Great American Revolution (Six Flags Magic Mountain), *vi*, 11, 19–20, 77
Great American Scream Machine (Six Flags): Great Adventure, 17, 87, 124; Over Georgia, 11, 15, 23, *32*, 80, **134–35**, *135*
Great Chase (Six Flags): America, 83; Elitch Gardens, 78; New England, 83
Great Coasters International, 27, 29
Great Escape (NY), 88, 116–17; Comet, 13–14, **43**, 88, *89*, **130**
Great Nor'Easter (Morey's Piers), 86
Great White: Morey's Piers, 86, *86*; Seaworld of Texas, 95

Green Slime Mine Car (Paramount's Great America), 76
Greezed Lightnin' (Six Flags Astroworld), 95
Grizzly (Paramount): Great America, 76; Kings Dominion, **44**, 97, **133**
Gwazi (Busch Gardens), 79

Hain, Clair, 27, 29
Hangman (Wild Adventures), 81
Hercules (Dorney Park), 92, *93*, 128
Hersheypark (PA), 92–93, 113; Lightning Racer, 27, 29, **45**, 92; Wildcat, *26*, 27, **47**, 135
High Roller: Stratosphere Tower, 85; Valleyfair, 84
High Speed Thrill Coaster (Knoebel's), 94
Hillcrest Park (IL), 81
Holiday World (IN), 81; Legend, **45**, 81, **127**; Raven, 45, **46**, 81, **127**, **132**
Hoosier Hurricane (Indiana Beach), 82
Howler (Holiday World), 81
Hurler (Paramount): Carowinds, 89, **130**; Kings Dominion, 97, **130**
Hurricane: Adventureland, 87; Myrtle Beach Pavilion, 95; Playland, 88; Santa Cruz Beach Boardwalk, 76
Hypersonic XLC (Paramount's Kings Dominion), 97

Ice Mountain Bobsled (Enchanted Forest), 91
Idaho, 81
Idlewild Park (PA), 94
Illinois, 81. *See also* Six Flags Great America
Incredible Hulk (Islands of Adventure), 80
Indiana, 81–82. *See also* Holiday World
Intamin, AG, 19–21, 48
Invertigo (Paramount's Great America), 76
Iowa, 82
Iron Dragon (Cedar Point), 90
Iron Wolf (Six Flags Great America), 25, 81, **124**
Islands of Adventure (FL), 80

Jack Rabbit: Bear Trax, 88; Clementon Lake Park, 86; Kennywood, 94, 113
Jaguar (Knott's Berry Farm), 76
Japan, 63–66. *See also* Nagashima Spaland
Jazzland (LA), 82
Jet Star II (Lagoon), 96
Joker's Jinx (Six Flags America), 83
Joker's Revenge (Six Flags Fiesta Texas), 96
Joust (Dutch Wonderland), 92
Joyland Amusement Park (KS), 82
Judge Roy Scream (Six Flags Over Texas), 96, *97*

Kansas, 82
Kennywood (PA), 15, 94, *94*, 111

Kentucky, 82. *See also* Six Flags Kentucky
    Kingdom
Kiddieland (IL), 81
King Cobra (Paramount's Kings Island), 11,
    18, 90
Kings Dominion (VA). *See* Paramount's
    Kings Dominion
Kings Island (OH). *See* Paramount's Kings
    Island
Knoebel's Amusement Park (PA), 94, 113;
    Phoenix, 15, 22, **45**, 94; Twister, **47**, 94
Knott's Berry Farm (CA), 11, 76, 103; Ghost
    Rider, **44**, 76
Kong (Six Flags Marine World), 77
Kraken (Seaworld), 80
Kumba (Busch Gardens), 25, **51**, 79, *79*

Lagoon (UT), 96
Lake Compounce (CT), 78, 116; Boulder
    Dash, **42**, 78, 116, **128**, **130**
Lakemont Park (PA), 6, 94
Lake Placid Bobsleds (Palisades Amusement
    Park), 12, 16
Lakeside Amusement Park (CO), 78, *78*
Lake Winnepesaukah (GA), 80
Larris, Denise Dinn, 25–26
Laser (Dorney Park), 92
Las Vegas (NV), 84–85
La Vibora (Six Flags Over Texas), 96
Leap the Dips (Lakemont Park), 6, 41, 94
Legend (Holiday World), **45**, 81, **127**
Le Monstre (La Ronde), 23, 74
Libertyland (TN), 95
Lightning Racer (Hersheypark), 27, 29, **45**,
    92, 113
Lil' Dipper (Camden Park), 98
Lil' Phantom (Kennywood), 94
Little Coaster (Arnolds Park), 82
Little Dipper: Hillcrest Park, 81; Kiddieland,
    81; Lakemont Park, 94
Little Eagle (Myrtle Beach Pavilion), 95
Little Laser (Dorney Park), 92
Loch Ness Monster (Busch Gardens), 17, 97,
    105
Looping Star, Brazil, 99; Oaks Amusement
    Park, 92
Louisiana, 82

Mabillard, Claude, 25
McNulty, Dennis, 26
Mad Mouse: Lakemont Park, 94; Myrtle
    Beach Pavilion, 95; Valleyfair, 84
Magic Kingdom (FL), 80
Magic Mountain (CA). *See* Six Flags Magic
    Mountain
Magic Springs (AR), 75
Magnum XL-200 (Cedar Point), **51**, **54**, 90,
    129, **132**, **133**; facts about, 57; history of,
    11, 17–18

Maine, 83
Mamba (Worlds of Fun), 84
Manhattan Express (New York Hotel and
    Casino), 18–19, 85, 124
Mantis (Cedar Point), 90, **122**, *123*
Maryland, 83, 105–6
Massachusetts, 83, 116. *See also* Six Flags
    New England
Matterhorn (Disneyland), 9, 16, 41, 75
Mayan Mindbender (Six Flags Astroworld),
    95
Mean Streak (Cedar Point), 90, 108, 128,
    133–34, *134*
Medusa (Six Flags): Great Adventure, 12, 25,
    28, **51**, 87; Marine World, **52**, 77
Mega Zeph (Jazzland), 82
Mexico, 74
Michigan's Adventure, 83; Shivering
    Timbers, **46**, 83
Mighty Canadian Minebuster (Paramount
    Canada's Wonderland), 74
Mild Thing (Valleyfair), 84
Millennium Force (Cedar Point), 12, **52**, 57,
    90, **130**, *131*, **131**
Miller, Chad, 25–26
Miller, John (John Miller Company), 6,
    15–16
Mind Bender: Galaxyland (Canada), 73; Six
    Flags Over Georgia, 20, *21*, **52**, 80
Mind Eraser (Six Flags): America, 83; Darien
    Lake, 88; Elitch Gardens, 78; New
    England, 83; Worlds of Adventure, 91
Mine Train (Six Flags Over Texas), 96
Mini Mine Train (Six Flags Over Texas), 96
Minnesota, 83–84
Miracle Strip Amusement Park (FL), 80
Missouri, 84, 110–11
Mr. Freeze (Six Flags Theme Parks), 60, 84,
    96, *98*
Monster Mouse (Oaks Amusement Park), 92
Montezooma's Revenge (Knott's Berry
    Farm), 76
Montu (Busch Gardens), 25, **53**, 79, **120**
Morey's Piers (NJ), 86
Morgan Manufacturing, 30
Mulholland Madness (Disney's California
    Adventure), 75
Muskrat Scramble (Jazzland), 82
Myrtle Beach Pavilion (NC), 95

Nagashima Spaland (Japan), **58**, 64; Steel
    Dragon, 30, **54**, 58, 64; White Cyclone, *47*
Nascar Café (NV), 85
Nevada, 84–85
New Hampshire, 85
New Jersey, 86–87, 114–15. *See also* Six Flags
    Great Adventure
New York, 87–88, 114–15, 116–19. *See also*
    Coney Island

New York Hotel and Casino (Las Vegas), 85; Manhattan Express, 18–19, 85, 124
Nightmare (Great Escape), 88, 117
Nightmare Mine (Frontier City), 91
Ninja (Six Flags): Magic Mountain, 17, 77, **128**; Over Georgia, 80; St. Louis, 84
Nitro (Six Flags Great Adventure), *viii, 53,* **53–54,** 87, **129, 131**
North Carolina, 89

Oaks Amusement Park (OR), 92
Ohio, 89–91, 108–10. *See also* Cedar Point; Paramount's Kings Island
Oklahoma, 91
Old Town (FL), 80
Oregon, 91–92
Orient Express (Worlds of Fun), 84
Outlaw (Adventureland), 82

Palisades Amusement Park (NJ), 8, 9, 12, 16
Paramount Canada's Wonderland, 74, 119, **129**
Paramount's Carowinds (NC), 89; Hurler, 89, **130**
Paramount's Great America (CA), 76; Vortex, 76, **124**
Paramount's Kings Dominion (VA), 58, **58,** 97, 105; Flight of Fear, 97, *99,* **126;** Grizzly, **44,** 97, **133;** Hurler, 97, **130;** Volcano the Blast Coaster, 97, **122**
Paramount's Kings Island (OH), 9, 11, 43, **58,** 90–91, 110; Adventure Express, 90, **124;** Flight of Fear, 90, **126;** King Cobra, 11, 18, 90; the Racer, 9, *10,* 11, 15, 58, 90; Son of Beast, 21, 25, 58, 91, 128; Top Gun, 17, 91, **128,** *129;* Vortex, 17, *17,* 91. *See also* Beast
Patriot (Castles and Coasters), 75
Pegasus (Big Chief Kart and Coaster World), 98
Pennsylvania, 92–95, 111–14. *See also* Dorney Park; Hersheypark; Knoebel's Amusement Park
Phantom's Revenge (Kennywood), 94, 112
Philadelphia Toboggan Coasters (PTC), 15
Phoenix (Knoebel's), 15, 22, **45,** 94
Pierce, John, 23–24
Playland: Canada, 73; New Jersey, 86; New York, 88
Pleasure Beach (England), **57,** 58, 69, 70
Poison Ivy's Twisted Train (Six Flags New England), 83
Poltergeist (Six Flags Fiesta Texas), 96
Predator (Six Flags Darien Lake), 88
Primeval Whirl (Disney's Animal Kingdom), 80
Prior, Frank, 6–7, 16, 27, 46
Psycho Mouse (Paramount's Great America), 76
Psyclone (Six Flags Magic Mountain), 14, 77

Pteranodon Flyers (Islands of Adventure), 80
Puff the Little Fire Dragon (Lagoon), 96
Python: Busch Gardens, 79; Playland, 86

Quantum Loop (Sea Breeze), 88

Racer: Kennywood, 94, *94,* 113; Paramount's Kings Island, 9, *10,* 11, 15, 58, 90
Raging Wolf Bobs, *7,* 22, 81, 91
Rampage (Visionland), **45,** 75
Raptor (Cedar Point), 25, **54,** 90, 108, **120**
Rattler (Six Flags Fiesta Texas), 24–25, 96
Raven (Holiday World), 45, **46,** 81, **127, 132**
RC-48 (Morey's Piers), 86
Rebbie, Tom, 15
Rebel Yell (Paramount's Kings Dominion), 97
Red Devil (Ghost Town in the Sky), 89
Revolution: Libertyland, 95; Six Flags Magic Mountain, *vi,* 11, 19–20, 77
Rex's Railrunner (Jazzland), 82
Ricochet: Paramount's Carowinds, 89; Paramount's Kings Dominion, 97
Riddler's Revenge (Six Flags Magic Mountain), 77, **122**
Ripper (Thrillville USA), 92
Ripsaw (Knott's Camp Snoopy), 83
River King Mine Ride (Six Flags St. Louis), 84
Riverside Cyclone (MA), 23, 24
Road Runner Express (Six Flags): Fiesta Texas, 96, **124;** Kentucky Kingdom, 82; Marine World, 77; Worlds of Adventure, 91
Road Runner Railway (Six Flags Great Adventure), 87
Roar (Six Flags): America, 83; Marine World, 27, *38,* **46,** 77
Roaring Twenties Corkscrew (Knott's Berry Farm), 11, 16
Rock and Roller Coaster (Disney-MGM Studios), 79, **126**
Roller Coaster Corporation of America (RCCA), 24–25
Roller Skater (Six Flags Kentucky Kingdom), 82
Roller Soaker (Hersheypark), 93
Rollies Coaster (Morey's Piers), 86
Rolling Thunder (Six Flags Great Adventure), 87
Rollo Coaster (Idlewild Park), 94
Rollschuhcoaster (Six Flags Fiesta Texas), 96
Rugrats Runaway Reptar (Paramount's Kings Island), 90
Runaway Mine Train (Six Flags Over Texas), 9, 96, **124**
Runaway Ore Cart (Silver Dollar City), 84
Runaway Train (Six Flags Great Adventure), 87

Santa Cruz Beach Boardwalk (CA), 76; Giant Dipper, 76, 77, 113, **135**

Scandia Family Fun Center (CA), 76

Schmeck, Herbert, 15

Schwarzkopf, Anton, 19–20, 52

Scooby Doo's Ghoster Coaster (Paramount): Canada's Wonderland, 74; Carowinds, 89; Kings Dominion, 97; Kings Island, 90

ScooperdooperLooper (Hersheypark), 93

Scorpion (Busch Gardens), 79

Screamin' Eagle (Six Flags St. Louis), 15, 23, 84, 110, **134**

Screechin' Eagle (Americana), 89

Sea Breeze (NY), 88, 118

Sea Dragon (Wyandot Lake), 91

Sea Serpent (Morey's Piers), 86

Seaworld (FL), 80

Sea World of Texas, 95

Serial Thriller: Six Flags Astroworld, 95; Six Flags Worlds of Adventure, 91

Serpent: Americana Amusement Park, 89; Six Flags Astroworld, 95

Shivering Timbers (Michigan's Adventure), **46**, 83

Shock Wave: Paramount's Kings Dominion, 97; Six Flags Great America, 81, 124; Six Flags Over Texas, 20, 96, 106

Sidewinder: Hersheypark, 93; Six Flags Elitch Gardens, 78

Silver Bullet (Frontier City), 91

Silver Dollar City (MO), 84; Thunderation, 84, **124**

Silver Streak (Paramount Canada's Wonderland), 74

Silverwood Theme Park (ID), 16, 81

Six Flags: season passes, 36. *See also* Batman—The Ride

Six Flags America (MD), 83, 105–6; Superman Ride of Steel, 55, 83

Six Flags Astroworld (TX), 95, 107; Texas Cyclone, 14, 23, 43–44, 95; Texas Tornado, 20, **55**, 95

Six Flags Darien Lake (NY), 88, 118–19; Superman Ride of Steel, 55, 88, 119

Six Flags Elitch Gardens (CO), 47, 78

Six Flags Fiesta Texas, 24–25, 96, 107; Road Runner Express, 96, **124**

Six Flags Great Adventure (NJ), **59**, 87, 114–15; Batman and Robin—the Chiller, **49**, 59, 60, 87, *87*, 115; Medusa, 12, 25, *28*, **51**; Nitro, *viii*, *53*, 53–54, 87, **129**, **131**; Viper, 18, *19*, 87

Six Flags Great America (IL), 81; Batman—The Ride, *24*, 25, 50, **50**, 81; Iron Wolf, 25, 81, **124**

Six Flags Kentucky Kingdom, 82; Chang, 82, **122**; Thunder Run, 82, **130**

Six Flags Magic Mountain (CA), 11, 18, **59**, 76–77, 102–3; Ninja, 17, 77, **128**;

Revolution, *vi*, 11, 19–20, 77; Riddler's Revenge, 77, **122**; Viper, 38, 77, 124

Six Flags Marine World (CA), 77; Medusa, **52**, 77; Roar, 27, *38*, **46**, 77

Six Flags New England (MA), 83, 116; Cyclone, **43**, 83, 116; Superman Ride of Steel, 20–21, **48**, 83, 116, **129**, **131**, **132**, **133**; Thunderbolt, 49, 83

Six Flags Over Georgia, 11, **59**, 80; Georgia Cyclone, 14, 22–23, **43–44**, 80; Great American Scream Machine, 11, 15, 23, *32*, 80, **134–35**, *135*; Mind Bender, 20, *21*, **52**, 80

Six Flags Over Texas, 8, 9, **59–60**, 96, 106; Judge Roy Scream, 96, *97*; Mr. Freeze, 60, 96; Runaway Mine Train, 9, 96, **124**; Texas Giant, 23, *42*, **46–47**, 96, **132**

Six Flags St. Louis (MO), 84, 110; Boss, **42**, 84, **127**; Mr. Freeze, 60, 84; Screamin' Eagle, 15, 23, 84, 110, **134**

Six Flags Worlds of Adventure (OH), **60**, 91, 109–10; Batman Knight Flight, **49**, 91; Big Dipper, 6, 60, 91, **130**

Skull Mountain (Six Flags Great Adventure), 87

Skyliner (Lakemont Park), 22, 94

Sky Princess (Dutch Wonderland), 92

Skyrider (Paramount Canada's Wonderland), 74

Son of Beast (Paramount's Kings Island), 21, 25, 58, 91, 128

South America, 99–100

South Carolina, 95

Spacely's Sprocket Rockets (Six Flags Great America), 81

Space Mountain: Disneyland, 75, **126**; Disney World, 80, **126**

Speed (Nascar Café), 85

Star Jet (Casino Pier), 86

Starliner (Miracle Strip), 80

Stealth Steel (Paramount's Great America), 76

Steamin' Demon (Great Escape), 88

Steel Dragon (Japan), 30, **54**, **58**, **61**

Steel Eel (Seaworld of Texas), 95

Steel Force (Dorney Park), 30, *39*, **54**, 92, **130**, **132**

Stengel, Werner, 10–21

Stratosphere Tower (NV), 85

Stricker's Grove (OH), 91

Summers, Curtis (Curtis Summers, Inc.), 21–23

Superman Krypton Coaster (Six Flags Fiesta Texas), 96

Superman Ride of Steel (Six Flags), 55; America, 83, 106; Darien Lake, 55, 88, 119; New England, 20–21, **48**, 83, 116, **129**, **131**, **132**, **133**

Superman—The Escape (Six Flags Magic Mountain), 77

Superman Ultimate Escape (Six Flags Worlds of Adventure), 91, 110
Superman Ultimate Flight (Six Flags Over Georgia), 80
Superstition Mountain (Indiana Beach), 82
Switchback Railway (Coney Island, New York), 4–5, 14

Talon (Dorney Park), 92
Taxi Jam (Paramount): Canada's Wonderland, 74; Carowinds, 89; Great America, 76; Kings Dominion, 97
Teddy Bear (Stricker's Grove), 91
Tennessee, 95
Tennessee Tornado (Dollywood), 95
Texas, 95–96, 106–7. *See also* Six Flags Astroworld; Six Flags Over Texas
Texas Cyclone (Six Flags Astroworld), 14, 23, 43–44, 95
Texas Giant (Six Flags Over Texas), 23, *42*, **46–47**, 96, **132**
Texas Tornado: Six Flags Astroworld, 20, **55**, 95; Wonderland, 96
Thompson, LaMarcus, 4, 5–6, 11
Thrillville USA (OR), 92
Thunderation (Silver Dollar City), 84, **124**
Thunderbolt: Kennywood, 94, 113; Six Flags New England, 49, 83
Thunderbolt Express (Camden Park), 98
Thunder Hawk (Dorney Park), 92
Thunder Road (Paramount's Carowinds), 89
Thunder Run (Six Flags Kentucky Kingdom), 82, **130**
Tiger Terror (Wild Adventures), 81
Tig'rr (Indiana Beach), 82
Timberline Twister (Knott's Berry Farm), 76
Timber Terror (Silverwood Theme Park), 81
Timber Wolf (Worlds of Fun), 22, 84
Titan (Six Flags Over Texas), 96
Togo International, 18–19
Top Cat's Tax Jam (Paramount's Kings Island), 91
Top Gun (Paramount): Canada's Wonderland, 74; Carowinds, 89; Great America, 76; Kings Island, 17, 91, **128**, *129*
Tornado: Adventureland, 82; Brazil, 99; Dollywood, 95; Oaks Amusement Park, 92; Six Flags Astroworld, 20, **55**, 95; Stricker's Grove, 91; Wonderland, 96
Trailblazer (Hersheypark), 93
Traver, Harry, 7, 16
Tremors (Silverwood Theme Park), 81
T2 (Six Flags Kentucky Kingdom), 82
Twist and Shout (Magic Springs), 75
Twisted Sisters (Six Flags Kentucky Kingdom), 82
Twister (Knoebel's), **47**, 94
Twister II (Six Flags Elitch Gardens), 78
Two Face (Six Flags America), 83, 106

Ultra Twister (Six Flags Astroworld), 18, 95
Underground (Adventureland), 82
Universal Studios Islands of Adventure (FL), 80
Utah, 96

Valleyfair (MN), 84
Vekoma International, 29–30
Villain (Six Flags Worlds of Adventure), 91
Viper (Six Flags): Astroworld, 95; Darien Lake, 88; Great Adventure, 18, *19*, 87; Great America, 14, 81; Magic Mountain, 38, 77, 124
Virginia, 97, 104–5. *See also* Paramount's Kings Dominion
Visionland (AL), 75; Rampage, **45**, 75
Volcano the Blast Coaster (Paramount's Kings Dominion), 97, **122**
Vortex (Paramount): Canada's Wonderland, 74, 119, **129**; Carowinds, 89; Great America, 76, **124**; Kings Island, 17, *17*, 91
V2 Vertical Velocity (Six Flags): Great America, 81; Marine World, 77

Wacky Worm: Lake Winnepesaukah, 80; Worlds of Fun, 84
Waldameer Park (PA), 94
Walt Disney World (FL). *See* Disney World
Washington, 98
Waterville USA (AL), 75
West Coaster (Pacific Pier), 76
Western Washington Fairgrounds, 98
West Virginia, 98
Whalom Park (MA), **133**
Whirlwind (Knoebel's), 94
White Cyclone (Japan), **47**, 58, 64
Whizzer (Six Flags Great America), 19, 81
Wicked Twister (Cedar Point), 57, 90, 109
Wild Adventures (GA), 81
Wildcat: Cedar Point, 90; Frontier City, 91; Hersheypark, *26*, *27*, **47**, 93, 113, **135**; Lake Compounce, 78, 116
Wild Chipmunk (Lakeside Amusement Park), 78
Wilde Beast (Paramount Canada's Wonderland), 74
Wilde Maus (Busch Gardens), 97
Wildfire (Silver Dollar City), 84
Wild Kitty (Frontier City), 91
Wild Mouse: Casino Pier, 86; Crystal Palace (Canada), 73; Dorney Park, 92; Hersheypark, 93; Idlewild Park, 94; Lagoon, 96; Playland, 86
Wild One (Six Flags America), 22, 83
Wild Thing (Valleyfair), 30, 84
Wile E. Coyote's Grand Canyon Blaster (Six Flags Over Texas), 96
Williams Grove (PA), 95
Windstorm (Old Town, FL), 80

Wisconsin, 98
Wizard's Cavern (Casino Pier), 86
Wolverine Wildcat (Michigan's Adventure),
    22, 83
Wonderland (TX), 96
Woodstock's Express: Cedar Point, 90;
    Dorney Park, 92
Worlds of Fun (MO), 84, 111
Wyandot Lake (OH), 91

X (Six Flags Magic Mountain), 18, 77
Xcelerator (Knott's Berry Farm), 76
X-Flight (Six Flags Worlds of Adventure), 91
XLR-8 (Six Flags Astroworld), 11, 95

Yankee Cannonball (Canobie Lake Park), 15,
    85

Zach's Zoomer (Michigan's Adventure), 83
Zeus (Big Chief Kart and Coaster World), 98
Zingo (Bell's Amusement Park), 91
Zippin Pippin (Libertyland), 95
Zoomerang (Lake Compounce), 78
Zydeco Scream (Jazzland), 82
Zyklon (Magic Springs), 75